THE SOVEREIGN TOUCH

God Is Either Sovereign Over All, or He Isn't Sovereign at All

THE SOVEREIGN TOUCH

God Is Either Sovereign Over All, or He Isn't Sovereign at All

by
John Enslow

Shulamite Ministries
Suches, Georgia

Statement of Faith

Providing a statement of faith has always seemed a little odd to me. As living epistles, our lives ARE our statements of faith. I live what I believe, and you should be able to look at my life and see what that is. This works perfectly in person, in churches, and in actual relationships. But when preparing to read someone's book, they aren't there in person and we need a quick reference to see if that author is playing for our team.

I don't think this needs to be complicated, so here is my very simple statement of faith:

Jesus Christ, the only begotten Son of God, came in the flesh, shed His Holy Blood on the Cross at Calvary for the sins of the world. He is Lord of the universe, King of Kings, and I am His.

Table of Contents

Foreword

In reading this book you will not meet theory or theology.
You will meet a real person, a man who had the courage
to face God for His answers to life's deepest question:
>Is God really in control over all
>the wrongs and suffering of this messy world?
>(or Does God really reign over all the wrongs....)

John brings a rich and broad answer to his question and yours.
He stands squarely on the scriptures to declare and to believe
the ultimate truth that God is God. And he lives on
the foundation of a robust relationship with Christ,
in the integrity of a raw and constant dialogue with
his personal Father.

John has lived this book.
He experienced firsthand, the Sovereign Touch.

This a true story, a private revelation from God revealing
Himself to one man who faced Him with stark questions.
The testimony of "the Sovereign Touch" is
this rare pronouncement: God is honored as God!

>*As a result people are without excuse.*
>*For though they knew God,*
>*they did not glorify Him as God...*
>*Romans 1:20b-21 HCSB*

In the end, the answer to the question
is a gift of awe and wonder.

God is sovereign and
God is unfathomable love.

Martha Kilpatrick

Experience the Sovereign Touch

Good when He gives, supremely good;
Nor less when He denies:
Afflictions, from His sovereign hand,
Are blessings in disguise.

Brother Lawrence
French Carmelite friar
1614 - 1691

The outward man does indeed suffer wear and tear,
but every day the inward man receives fresh strength.
2 Corinthians 4:16 Phillips

What is Sovereignty and Why Should I Care?

What is sovereignty? What does it mean to serve a Sovereign God? Grappling with these questions is normal and a natural part of the process to accept Jesus' lordship in our lives. Without that wrestling, I am not certain there can be a true surrender to a Sovereign God. To yield our will—we have to face it down and push back against our natural rebellion. And while embracing a Sovereign God costs us everything, only by doing so are we ushered into the true victory of Christ's Life. So, what does it mean that God is sovereign?

Remember the things I have done in the past. For I alone am God! I am God, and there is none like me. Only I can tell you the future before it even happens. Everything I plan will come to pass, for I do whatever I wish. I will call a swift bird of prey from the east—a leader from a distant land to come and do my bidding. I have said what I would do, and I will do it.
Isaiah 46:9-11 NLT

God telling us exactly what His sovereignty means. A Sovereign God has the "absolute right to govern all things as He chooses, without any limitations imposed by circumstances or human choices."[1] And at the same time, God is *not* a bully.

Sovereignty is a reality that few wish to tackle because the ramification of it in our lives is enormous. This is not just another Christian doctrine we can pick up and flash – like a merit badge; embracing sovereignty is embracing true Lordship. And once I bow to Jesus as Lord, He's revealed to be Lord over the entirety of my life, and not just from that moment. Why else would countless people resist embracing

---

1 Revell Concise Bible Dictionary Fleming H. Revell Company, Tarrytown, NY. Copyright 1990, p. 513.

the reality of sovereignty?

Deep in our core, we know that if God truly is sovereign, we would have to face the truth; that painful things happened to us and He did not prevent them. Sovereignty goes beyond ending my rule over life; it yields and makes peace with God's rule over my ALL—my blessings and my failures, my joy and my suffering.

Our God is involved. He is completely involved—even when I do not agree or understand. Yet God is never going to satisfy my demands that He give an account of His Sovereign rule. So I can either reject God utterly, or surrender to Him as Sovereign, bowing to His ways and His choices. God does not owe me an explanation for my suffering. But if I bow to His sovereign hand, He just might reveal to me His divine purpose and plan for all of my story.

The LORD works out everything to its proper end — even the wicked for a day of disaster.
Proverbs 16:4 NIV

For in Him all things were created: things in heaven and on earth, visible and invisible, whether thrones or powers or rulers or authorities; all things have been created through Him and for Him.
Colossians 1:16 NIV

THE POTTER AND HIS CLAY

What should we say then? Is there injustice with God? Absolutely not! For He tells Moses:
I will show mercy to whom I will show mercy, and I will have compassion on whom I will have compassion.
So then it does not depend on human will or effort but on God who shows mercy. For the Scripture tells Pharaoh:

I raised you up for this reason so that I may display My power in
you and that My name may be proclaimed in all the earth.
So then, He shows mercy to those He wants to, and He hardens
those He wants to harden.
You will say to me, therefore, "Why then does He still find fault?
For who can resist His Will?" But who are you, a mere man, to
talk back to God? Will what is formed say to the one who formed it,
"Why did you make me like this?" Or has the potter no right over
the clay, to make from the same lump one piece of pottery for honor
and another for dishonor? And what if God, desiring to display
His wrath and to make His power known, endured with much pa-
tience objects of wrath ready for destruction? And what if He did
this to make known the riches of His glory on objects of mercy that
He prepared beforehand for glory — on us, the ones He also called,
not only from the Jews but also from the Gentiles? As He also says
in Hosea:
I will call Not My People, My People, and she who is Unloved,
Beloved. And it will be in the place where they were told, you are
not My people, there they will be called sons of the living God.
Romans 9:14-26 HCSB

WHAT GOD ALLOWS

Have you ever heard someone say, "Why does God allow so
much pain and suffering?" I have always believed in God's
"allowance" of hurtful things in my life. By defining painful
situations as what God "allows," I am able to separate Him
from the pain rather than blaming Him for it. But God allowing something is quite different from Him *orchestrating* life.
"Allowing" implies that God is Lord through passive proxy,
not by sovereign right. In actuality, God works all things together to produce His Will. My pain is not without purpose.

Woven by God, the fabric of our lives includes some very
painful threads. Some have caused us great grief, a lifetime

of crisis. His shuttle passes through our lives with purposed threads to weave a tapestry more amazing than we could ever know. And while some cords were—and still are—awful to experience, they are each intended to glorify. If we look at these threads one by one, they are hard to accept, but as part of the great sovereign work God is unfolding…they can be beautiful.

It is my response to suffering that sows either bitterness and resentment or fruitfulness and benefit in my life. I was not promised pain-free living and neither were you. No one said that calamity would not befall us.

I could give you a list of my personal tragedies and you could do the same for me – this is our life. But here is the kicker: Can I see all of life, including these heartbreaks, in the Light of God's purposed work? In other words, can I see His blessing in them, or do I only feel His neglect?

Accepting the pain of your life is a path of growth and expansion; fighting it inevitably leads to bitterness.

Are you stuck? Are there whole areas of your life that just do not change? The bitter belief that God is not good will stunt your growth as a person and limit your life. Until you reckon with God's sovereignty, your bitterness will poison you and everyone around you.

If you are willing to enter the mystery, and embrace sovereignty, then you can release yourself into God's hands. You will discover that you are completely cared for and totally known—not in spite of—but because of your hardships.

Resisting this only causes us to lose the benefits God intends us to gain through that pain. We will feel the ache regardless (the pain is real), but it would be foolish to miss our Reward out of ingratitude and rebellion.

As you purpose to trust God with your whole life, He will be able to move all about you and through you to produce *fullness.*

THE SOVEREIGN JOURNEY

Laying out this book I start with ground zero of our personal sovereign experience. It is here in the microcosm where sovereignty touches our individual lives and circumstances. I proceed by expanding our view of the Sovereign Touch to the macrocosm by extending out to family, local authority, national government, and finally the world. My goal is to illustrate God's sovereign rule – and the blessing that comes when we embrace it. If God is truly sovereign, then the whole gamut of life is orchestrated by Him.

In my experience, people tend to be mostly interested in how sovereignty personally affects their lives. Childhood abuse? I intend on looking at that. What about things that crippled us emotionally, physically, mentally, and spiritually? That, too, we will address and explore. When talking about God's sovereignty, the most visceral reaction is to our pain and why God "allowed" it. Yes, I will look at this as well.

I will not be addressing sovereignty like some cold academic because I am not a scholar or theologian. In these pages, I share my personal wrestling match with God and His sovereignty. None of us are exempt from God's sovereign touch, for He is The Sovereign. We do, however, have a choice to embrace God's sovereignty or to deny Him.

I pray that through this book, the Lord will reveal to you the trustworthiness of His sovereign hand. I pray that the Spirit expands your universe to include all of life not just what you will accept. Embracing God's Sovereignty is a work of abandonment to your Creator and will usher you into the joy of full surrender. In this acceptance, you will experience true Lordship, not just assent to its creed.

We wish you could see how all this is working out for your benefit, and how the more grace God gives, the more thanksgiving will redound to His glory. This is the reason why we never collapse. The outward man does indeed suffer wear and tear, but every day the inward man receives fresh strength. These little troubles (which are really so transitory) are winning for us a permanent, glorious and solid reward out of all proportion to our pain. For we are looking all the time not at the visible things but at the invisible. The visible things are transitory: it is the invisible things that are really permanent.
2 Corinthians 4:15-18 Phillips

Where Was God in the Pain of My Story?

When you go through a trial,
the sovereignty of God is the pillow
upon which you lay your head.

Charles H. Spurgeon
British pastor and author know as the "Prince of Preachers"
1834 - 1892

"As for you, you meant evil against me, but God meant it
for good, to bring it about that many people should be kept
alive, as they are today."
Genesis 50:20 EVS

The Dilemma of Sovereignty

I have had the privilege of walking in life and working with Martha Kilpatrick and Shulamite Ministries for over twenty-five years now.

As a young woman, Martha came face-to-face with her desperate need for God. Martha knew that she did not have the love for Him that He requires in His Word (See Matthew 22:37). Through an earnest seeking, the Lord graciously answered her quandary by revealing Himself as The Sovereign Lord over her entire life. This powerful message—even now—resonates through her teaching. Since I first heard her teachings, the echoes of that message has reverberated in my heart.

Through a brilliant and unique writing style, the Lord gave Martha a poignant way to communicate His messages. Her books have captivated many a seeking heart. It has been my privilege to assist her to get the messages out in front of as many people as possible.

I came to Shulamite Ministries to be discipled for the mission field. But the Lord had a different plan. His path led me to the participation of developing and expanding an international ministry with an online bookstore and multiple, multi-media websites. We just never know what the Father has in mind. We can make our plans, but the Lord determines our steps (Proverbs 16:9 NLT).

Along the way I have learned many things from the Lord through Martha, but one of my major lessons has been that God is in control and I am not.

Even though I am a child of God and a citizen of the Kingdom, I have very little control over life events. Yes, I have free will and can run roughshod over my life with it, but at the end of the day, God's sovereignty trumps all. God is sovereign and that means He rules over *everything*. I may maintain an illusion of dominion over my life, but what I am in fact vulnerable to is God's sovereignty. The surprise is that I am protected by it at the same time.

Martha has often said about sovereignty, "Everything in the world is exactly as it should be, or God would change it. And He can, He is God!" She references Romans 8:28:

And we know that God causes all things to work together for good to those who love God, to those who are called according to His purpose.
Romans 8:28

The Word says that God causes all things to work together for the good of those who *love* Him. What it does not say is that God will "work together" everything to make me happy. Sovereignty is a hard pill to swallow if you have not surrendered your life to His Lordship. And even after you surrender, it's no cakewalk.

I have witnessed many believers function as if they were God's only child, demanding and declaring an illegitimate power over everything. But for the child of God, sovereignty is safety. The true child of God is at the mercy of His Will and grace. This reality makes me safer than I have ever been in the entire course of my life, but also more dependent on and vulnerable to His grace and goodness.

This is why I believe that son-ship and sovereignty work in conjunction. Only a son can truly accept His Father's sovereign will. And there are not many sons, but one Son, Christ

Jesus, with one Body incorporating many members. Only One mind embraces the sovereign plan of God. I can comply with God's will, but to accept and embrace His sovereign choice? That comes from Another's Life. Sovereignty is the Will of the Father and accepting it is found in the Life of His Son.

No matter what happens, always be thankful, for this is God's will for you who belong to Christ Jesus.
1 Thessalonians 5:18 TLB

The Lord reigns! He is robed in majesty; The Lord is robed, enveloped in strength. The world is firmly established; it cannot be shaken.
Psalms 93:1 HCSB

God's Sovereignty, His Choice

God's sovereignty is a life or death issue. I have heard it preached that if Jesus is not Lord of your life, then it is not possible for you to be His disciple. And if lordship and discipleship are synonymous, then– it is important for us to see the issue of His sovereignty, which is Him ruling as Lord. In order for us to be under the Lordship of Christ, we have to embrace His sovereign moves. It is impossible for Jesus to be our Lord in reality and truth without accepting Him as sovereign over my life.

I want to delve into a hindrance, if not *the* hindrance, to receiving God's sovereignty in our personal lives: entitlement. Being entitled puts blinders on our eyes. Entitlement demands "what I deserve!" rather than receiving God's choice for my life. If I am looking to get what I think I *deserve*, I will never see what God is actually giving me.

Entitlement is a closed fist demanding it to be done *my way*. Embracing His Sovereign Touch comes open-handed receiving His choices. Entitlement and the embrace of God's sovereignty cannot coexist.

Disappointment awaits all entitled people. Why? Because entitlement judge circumstances with little to no understanding of His higher plan. The surprise is – often our sovereign blessings come to us through a different avenue than we would desire.

In a culture where everyone is raised to get a ribbon and all are deemed winners, where everyone is so special that no one is unique, we feel entitled to get what we want (or more, what we feel we deserve). This is a deadly mindset. So often God's sovereign move works counter to my own demands.

But because He is my Lord, I must choose to embrace His Ways. Therefore how do I embrace His Sovereign Touch? I do it through a choice to yield and trust. Because He is my Lord—and it cannot be done otherwise—I must choose to embrace His Ways. The people of God must live by the ways of God.

The Word says, "Anyone who is not with Me is against Me, and anyone who does not gather with Me scatters" (Matthew 12:30 GNT). We need to surrender and yield to His Lordship, rather than bowing out our chest to resist.

This is war, and there is no neutral ground. If you're not on My side, you're the enemy; if you're not helping, you're making things worse.
Matthew 12:30 MSG

Lordship is God being LORD! A true Lord makes ALL the choices over the subjects of His kingdom. Though I can pray and petition God for what I need and desire, my demands of Him are negligible. If Jesus being my Lord is made evident through being His disciple, then my feeling entitled to have things done my way should be a red flag that I am not actually surrendering to His sovereignty. God's sovereignty is about Him *being* Lord, and my being a disciple is about me *needing* a Lord.

Surrender to My Story

One of the major struggles in this life is to accept and embrace our God-given story. It is such a deep work and one that separates the men from the boys. To stand in the face of your God and receive the story He sovereignly authored for you is daunting.

Next is to be humble enough to bow and ask forgiveness for all the sinful choices we made in response to His choosing. Oh, and then to accept the blood of Jesus Christ as the only answer for those choices we made—that's a pride crusher. But the work of salvation, redemption, and sanctification is the greatest adventure!

There are many aspects to my life that I've resisted. Basically, I've struggled with the general landscape He created. I would have chosen for myself quite differently than He did. Because I'm so myopic, I can usually only judge by my feelings ("This didn't make me feel good, so it must be wrong").

What I'm learning of God's Purpose and Authorship of life is that it's all for Jesus. The Father is about glorifying His Son, and I have the privilege of being a benefactor of this process. At salvation, my story became His story. So now my story is not first for *me*, although it entirely includes me. Imagine this: the process of the Son's glorification includes my own sanctification. And in this we are made ONE. When we are vulnerable to God's sovereignty, we glorify Him. The breach I created through resisting my story is bridged by the ultimate price that Christ paid and in the Father's glorification of His Son.

While thinking about this, I went back and read the section on "Joseph" in Martha Kilpatrick's book, *All and Only*. Oh, how perfectly it lays out this whole process of accepting God's sovereign choices. Here is a barn burner quote: "Your suffering holds the secrets to your appointed lot and is therefore the hiding place of your power." The fact that God's choices can lead to our pain is undeniable, but bowing to His Will in how He chose to lay it out brings Life. My embrace of God as sovereign Lord of my story gives me a rich treasure chest of living power.

My Story Needs a Yes

A friend once said to me, "I'm learning the importance of saying yes to my story, because it's only in my story that He has a yes to me." Our surrender is paramount to actually living in this life. I told a beloved brother that giving God a blanket "Yes!" to the whole of life would make the process so much easier. I don't understand it all, but it's like greasing the wheels of our acceptance. God loves the blank check we write to Him! That blanket YES gives us a VIP pass through the process, like a skip-the-line pass they now have at amusement parks. No waiting in line, just go up to the front. It's worth the price at the parks, and it's worth even more in receiving your story.

So the Son is glorified in my life as I accept Him as Author and receive His Will for me. Wow! Let me give another powerful quote by Martha that paints quite a picture:

"There aren't many Josephs. We would rather pet our bitterness than wear a crown. And that is precisely our choice…"

I Called It Harsh

The Lord is ever working into me an acceptance of my story. I have kicked against His forming of me for, well, the majority of my life. I used to see the Father's thumb impression in my clay mass as a harsh and sometimes abusive thing. I may not have consciously attributed it to Him, but at my core, He's the one I faulted. And rightly so — He uses what He uses, to make us who He makes us. He is God, after all!

God circumstantially set me apart at birth. I was an only child and alone much of my life. I have been encapsulated unto Him all my life. Even when I did not call Him Lord, He set things up to hide me in sometimes violent ways. And I do not think this is something peculiar to me. God is a jealous God because of His intense Love, and He works things in all our lives to make us ever face Him. You do not have to be an only child to feel set apart. Who of us has not felt this separation?

This separating work makes us feel "off" or weird, and I think it is more common than not. The key here is until we know it is His Sovereign Touch, we do not know we are being separated "unto Him." All our loneliness is just being alone and not a Divine Touch.

I have often believed that if I did not have a steady flow of people interacting with *me*, that I was somehow strange. But this has been my situation more often than not.

Yes, my life's greatest desire to be acknowledged has been thwarted by Supernatural Neglect. I have largely existed under a painful and fiery cloak of invisibility and this was God's choice for me.

God wants us to want Him and we ever want something else. Let me not generalize and speak for you here, but this has certainly been true of me; I want to be heard, seen, and appreciated—not as great or brilliant, just as a person with a life and a voice. And God has made sure I have been…but mostly by Him alone.

My response to this calling has in the past been bitterness and pain. I fostered a bitterroot judgment against friends and family for what God Himself had orchestrated. Silly, I know, but oh-so-human. Imagine blaming the world for what God Himself has purposely withheld! He shelved me in the Potter's closet for His good purpose. Does that make me feel *special*? No, it often feels like rejection, and actually rejection has quite frequently been the force pushing me back onto my shelf. Yep, I have called His love a prison, and it has been. I am the Lord's prisoner, bars or no bars. We all are captured into the Lord's idea of us, and if we resist, it is a prison – a solitary confinement in the walls of His thinking.

Oh, the Sovereign Lord of our life and me, His captured one. I have the choice of response: bitterness or welcome. The walls remain unchanged, but my receptivity adjusts the climate: from dark and dingy to free and living. I do have the power to make it what I will.

Each day I choose to see His Will as loving and accepting. I can't say how I will respond tomorrow, but I open myself up to His today!

Our God is in heaven; He does whatever pleases Him.
Psalm 115:3 NIV

All the peoples of the earth are regarded as nothing. He does as He pleases with the powers of heaven and the peoples of the earth. No

one can hold back His hand or say to Him: "What have you done?"
Daniel 4:35 NIV

But who are you, a human being, to talk back to God? "Shall what
is formed say to the one who formed it, 'Why did you make me like
this?'"
Romans 9:20 NIV

Withholding and Beholding

What I would like to explore now is how we are affected when those who matter most deny us of what we think we need. How am I to respond when my key relationships fail to meet my crucial desires? What am I to do when father, mother, sister, brother, teacher, pastor fails me, in the office or role they hold? How do I respond when it seems these individuals are more a statement of what has been withheld, rather than what is given?

A father and mother's love, the shepherding pastor, and the camaraderie of a sibling are all interpersonal relationships that matter the most in our formative years. Then as we grow up, friends, boy/girlfriends, and spouses take their place. All these are seen as sources of life. So how do I respond when these key relationships feel more like betrayal than benefit? The answer is found at the Source.

When these disappointments occur, we must know there is a higher Purpose active there. This apparent withholding is for my beholding of Him. A greater Mind is at work. God's doing something that is beyond my seeing and feeling. And my need is to ask what, not why, but *what* are You after here, God?

I return to Martha Kilpatrick's chapter about Joseph in *All and Only*. Joseph's dilemma was not why God was allowing things to happen, but what He was forming through what He was doing. Joseph's questioning of God did not target His sovereignty, but purposed to bow to it instead. "What are You after? What are You looking to achieve through these circumstances You have created?"

It's a brave man who faces the facts laid out by his Sovereign

God. They remain facts whether we acknowledge and embrace them or not. But it's quite a courageous undertaking to ask the Sovereign Lord what He is after by allowing painful circumstances in this life.

"My father abandoned me. My mother scorned me. My siblings abused me. My pastor used me." These are the types of extremely painful situations that leave a lasting effect. We can choose to blame and complain about how these key figures have wronged us. We can ask God why He did this to us. Or we can bow like Joseph and ask, "What were You trying to bring about?" One stance yields while the other demands. One side of the coin is entitlement (I don't deserve this!) and the other is humility (I pray for understanding).

...to provide for those who mourn in Zion;
to give them a crown of beauty instead of ashes,
festive oil instead of mourning,
and splendid clothes instead of despair.
And they will be called righteous trees,
planted by the Lord to glorify Him.
Isaiah 61:3 HCSB

Gift of Wounding

One of my hopes is that the Holy Spirit uses this book to widen and enlighten our view of the pain, suffering, and wounds that we incurred at the hands of those with whom we had early, formative relationships. Many of these hurts are like an engram on our souls – scars that mark us as fallen in a fallen world. Though we may recover our autonomy, the effects of some of these wounds may leave a permanent limp in our gait.

When we have been wounded, one of our first impulses is to look for someone to pay for our affliction, someone to blame. Blame, rage, revenge, retaliation – all of these are common human reactions.

But the person who trusts and knows God eventually takes the agony of wounding to God. Their questioning comes to center on what the Lord is after in our spiritual maturing, rather than why God did not prevent the wound, or even why God caused it. A yielding spirit, rather than a demanding spirit, is the result. The questions of "what" and "why" face God's sovereignty in an open-hearted receiving of God's Lordship in our lives.

God's sovereignty is a reality that scares us to the core of our being. It can either be a bitter pill or a comforting proof of His Lordship and love. God's sovereignty tests our faith, even after we come to know God as perfectly good. We need His goodness as we learn to rest in His huge, loving hands.

It is normal and primal to fear God's sovereignty. "If the Master of the Universe chooses to work painful situations into my life, then I am the most vulnerable of all creatures. If He does not save me from pain but uses that pain instead, then I am truly at His mercy." What a frightening scenario in which to find ourselves!

It is easy to equate pain with the absence of love. The next natural progression in this line of thinking is to assume that if my Creator worked pain in my life, He does not love me. And if He does not love me, what hope do I have?

Biblically and theologically this is an ill-informed way of viewing our pain, but even when our view is checked or challenged, our fearful hearts are not pacified. Having anyone in control of my life and pain is daunting. And most of us, if we are honest, prefer to control our own lives than to accept God's sovereignty.

How do we free ourselves of angry reactions? The biblical character Jacob discovered this secret. Jacob, who would ultimately become God's man, started out as a sneaky, scheming, selfish man, and had done some things of which he was ashamed. While returning to his homeland to confront the jealous twin brother against whom he had sinned, he prepared lavish gifts in hopes of appeasement, secured the overnight safety of his wives, children and belongings, and camped alone overnight. The Bible tells us:

> *...a man wrestled with him until daybreak. When the man saw that he could not overpower him he touched the socket of Jacob's hip so that his hip was wrenched as he wrestled with the man. Then the man said, "Let me go, for it is daybreak." But Jacob replied, "I will not let you go unless you bless me."*
> *The man asked him, "What is your name?"*
> *"Jacob," he answered.*
> *Then the man said, "Your name will no longer be Jacob, but Israel, because you have struggled with God and with humans and have overcome."*

Jacob said, "Please tell me your name."
But he replied, "Why do you ask my name?" Then he blessed him
there.
So Jacob call the place Peniel, saying, "It is because I saw God face
to face, and yet my life was spared."
Genesis 32:24-30

A bruising encounter with God caused such a change in
Jacob that he needed a new name to fit his new character.
He had "overcome," been healed of his wounds – by God's
loving sovereign touch.

We, too, will experience true wholeness when we can see
our wounds through the lens of God's crippling touch to
the thigh of our strength – a great gift of His love, and not a
damaging curse.

A sermon by Derek Prince in which he discussed the sovereign majesty of God underscores this point:

"One of the essential requirements for being able to receive
Biblical prophecy is a right appreciation of the sovereignty,
the majesty, and the justice of God. God is always just. He
never makes mistakes; everything He does is right. Some
of you have been going through situations where you have
been wondering whether God wasn't making a mistake or
being unfair. But that's a wrong attitude."

I think this is always our temptation—to assume God is
making a mistake or is being unfair. But unfortunately, we
do not come to understand His ways by questioning His
sovereignty. We look to Him, bow to His sovereign hand,
and then we begin to understand His ways.

Another biblical character, a pagan king named Nebuchadnezzar, discovered the truth of God's sovereignty after a humiliating fall from power that left him insane, chomping grass in a field like an animal.

But at the end of those days, I, Nebuchadnezzar, looked up to heaven, and my sanity returned to me. Then I praised the Most High and honored and glorified Him who lives forever: For His dominion is an everlasting dominion, and His kingdom is from generation to generation. All the inhabitants of the earth are counted as nothing, and He does what He wants with the army of heaven and the inhabitants of the earth. There is no one who can hold back His hand or say to Him, "What have You done?"
Daniel 4:34-35 HCSB

The Plight of the Vulnerable

Perhaps it is the plight of the suffering, abused vulnerable ones among us – the children, the elderly, the disabled – that stirs our anger the most as we consider this matter of God's sovereignty.

The Lord sees these "little ones" whether anyone else does or not. I know many people who were neglected in their upbringing. Their parents were too involved in their own lives to be involved in their children's. This common scenario is played out in songs like Harry Chapin's "Cat's in the Cradle." It is altogether too easy for people to see their children as fixtures, not persons.

This is not, however, the case with our God. He *sees us* and *wants us to know it*.

In fact, God is passionately jealous to be known. Does that surprise you? Human jealousy is plagued with all that is fallen, sinful, and selfish. But God's jealousy is holy, righteous, and completely untainted with selfishness. He sees us with all of His deeply passionate, loving desire, not as fixtures or burdens, but as the apple of His eye. He wishes to tear us from all that prevents us from experiencing Him.

God's ways are not my ways. And this includes His jealousy. When we suffer or go through difficult circumstances, we usually take the opportunity to blame others, but what if God is the one to blame? What if our circumstances are the result of His jealousy? What if the wounding we received in our early years is more about God's desire and jealousy for our unadulterated affections than man's neglect? What if God did not give these parents eyes to see their children?

Provocative thoughts, for sure! But when God's sovereignty rubs up against our wounds, I am faced with a choice of whether to reject or receive His choice and Lordship.

I am not claiming that this is easy by any means. Neither am I excusing the neglect or abuse of a child – and God most certainly does not, either. That is the paradox. This whole dialogue – this grappling with my accusations and victim-hood, and yielding my control back to God – must be with Him. To see God's jealousy as punitive is to miss the whole point. He does not look at us like a taskmaster looks, with angry, accusing eyes. His eyes are filled with passion and longing for my whole heart.

The experience of the Lord's jealousy has annihilated my wayward pursuits and united me to Him as my Father, Husband, Beloved and Savior. The Father's jealousy is a jealousy against all that would destroy us, bring us into His infinite pleasure.

I have no problem grasping my own desire to know God, but to comprehend that I am known and seen by Him? This is more difficult. I can picture Him inspecting me for flaws, but delighting to be with me?

I often drive Martha Kilpatrick to conferences, appointments, and to getaways so that she can find quietness to write. On one such trip, God told Martha something that amazed me. He said that He just wanted to spend time with her during her time away. God was not looking for work, productivity, study, or even prayer from Martha. He simply wanted to spend time with her, to sit with her. Wow!

We are seen by our Father. He sees us with all of His deeply passionate desire. This is a gift beyond words and into Life.

But I was a CHILD!

Oh, the dreaded plight of the vulnerable. How many times have I screamed out at God, "I was a child, how could You have allowed this?"

Nothing over the years has given me a stronger platform to judge the "fairness" of God's sovereignty than my presumed innocence. My fiery anger against God blazed up because He allowed my suffering. "I asked for Your help, and You didn't help me!"

The next step towards the end of this short plank was to find out that my pain was not just allowed by Him – it was planned.

God's sovereignty is an all-or-nothing proposition. I am not saying I am happy about this truth, but it is the reality. And even when I have tried to refute it by rationalization, He is still sovereign. God is sovereign – whether I yield to His Sovereign Touch or not.

The only way I can embrace God's Sovereign Touch on my life is to view it through the lens of His goodness. Every other assessment is flawed and will lead me to bitterness. The thing about sovereignty is that even after I choose to accept it, I can still remain its martyr, seeing God's control as further abuse. This, too, is a slippery slope because it is also an accusation against God. Straight up, God's acts have to be judged by His character. There is no other way.

I have to see that behind God's sovereign hand is His loving heart, or I will become bitter.

No one can convince anyone else that the goodness of God.

It underlies His Sovereign Touch in our lives. Intellectual understanding may precede bowing to His sovereignty, but it does not replace a genuine willingness to yield one's spirit. Every wise character in the Bible—remember Daniel, David, Joseph and Job – yielded to God's sovereignty in the midst of their suffering. Only then were they given wisdom and the blessing held in sorrow's hands.

God's sovereignty provokes our will to build our faith. God's sovereignty challenges our willfulness in order to make us pliable to live. God's sovereignty is a request to bow to the Eternal King. God's sovereignty invites us into relationship with a God who works all things together for the good of those who love Him. And lastly sovereignty is Love!

Seen in the light of God's Love, our wounds from the hands of those who raised us, are more about our formation than we knew. Surrendering to His Sovereign Touch, these scars can be our making and not our curse. They can be a vehicle to bring us to Him, rather than a prod for pushing us away.

We know that all things work together for the good of those who love God: those who are called according to His purpose.
Romans 8:28 HCSB

A Call To The Heights

Every human being has an innate drive to live. Hold me under water for just a few seconds and watch me fight to breathe. Yet God has entrusted us to worship in and through our pain, in ways that completely counter our natural instinct to survive.

Let me demonstrate the sheer power and force of what is unleashed when we worship God in our pain, rather than lashing out in anger and despair.

It was the morning of October 17, 2000, a beautiful fall day. The long summer was over, the air was crisp and clean, the sky was remarkably blue, and the North Georgia Mountains were displaying a beautiful array of color.

My phone rang; it was my neighbor and co-worker, Martha Kilpatrick. With stress in her voice she said, "Can you help us get ready? Robyn has been in a car accident, and we need to get there as soon as possible." Robyn, the wife of Martha's eldest son, Scott, was an attractive and exquisite woman with a delightful smile and an elegant presence.

I rushed to Martha's home, prepared to help her and her husband Kenneth get ready to drive to Scott's. She greeted me at the door and began telling me what we needed to do when the phone rang. I will never forget those moments following that ring. Time seemed to slow.

I stood patiently, waiting for Martha to address the caller and hang up. But I watched as pain and anguish began to cover her face. I knew then that Robyn had not survived the crash. Later we discovered that her internal injuries were extensive and she had not survived the crash.

Paralyzed, I watched as tears streamed down Martha's face. She hung up the phone and threw it into a chair. As she fell to the floor, she screamed repeatedly, "Oh God, I praise You!"

For the next several minutes I watched as Martha bowed her will to the God she trusted. I was witnessing a transaction where she forcibly yielded her right to understand or even survive what she had just heard. Watching, I did not dare to intrude on this holy ground. I just witnessed as Martha transacted with her Heavenly Father!

Over the hours, days and months that followed, I saw in Martha, Scott, and the rest of the family in amazing grace and presence that was nothing less than supernatural. Pain and tears were not absent, but for a season the devastation of having a young woman plucked from the prime of life was not evident. I attribute this to the transaction that took place between Martha and God in those first few minutes of the crisis.

When we thank God and release an event to His sovereign plan, God is free to move on the situation; He is given ownership of what is already His. Martha's interaction with God was worship. No, there was no singing or organ music or liturgy, but there was a Gethsemane bowing. Is that not the true purpose of worship – to bow before the King of Kings?

As we journey through this fallen world, where none of us is given a pass for pain-free living, the Master of all is not unaffected or uninvolved with our suffering. God knows our agonies, and needs only the entrée of our worship to invite Him into each situation. We are the stewards of our lives, but He is the *life*. The difference between inviting Him into our circumstances and wrestling it out in frustration in our own strength is the difference between Light and darkness.

Martha's response on that clear autumn day was not a Pollyanna approach. In the Garden of Gethsemane, Christ sweat blood. Those drops were His offering of worship in that horrific reality as He faced the crucifixion.

True worship is not simply smiles and joyful singing. It is a ruthless demand, with no compromise, that our flesh bow to God as Sovereign.

What Happens if I Resist God's Sovereignty?

It is necessary – even crucial – for you to stand on the power and goodness of God because that is what humanity doubts and Satan attacks.

Martha Kilpatrick
Author, teacher, speaker and head of Shulamite Ministries

Look beneath the surface so you can judge correctly.
John 7:24 TPT

WHO WRITES MY STORY?

Our choices affect our destinies, but ultimately, the Author of my story is God. God writes all of our stories – because they are really HIStory. We cannot escape the script our Author has penned. We can resist, rebel, or kick against it, but it is our script, our story, and HIStory regardless.

God has designed us to be dependent on Him, to need Him. Our fight, because of the sin nature in each of us that resulted from Adam and Eve's disobedience, is to be independent of God and others. "I'll do it myself, thank you!"

But God, as the Author of HIStory, set up our lives so that we would eventually come to see our need for Him, and seek Him.

A Living Narrative

Walking through this world, we do not just meet people – we meet their deeply personal and extensive storylines. We greet living narratives with timelines, years of choices, and personal history. We never simply meet a two-dimensional facade; we encounter a complex stacking of events and background.

We may not wish for others to see below the surface of our lives, but it is not really hard to glimpse some of the choices people have made in life. Some of our common expressions give credence to this truth: "He looks rode hard and put up wet," or "He has such a stone-cold countenance," or "She's like a ray of sunshine, lighting up the room!"

Even if behind our veils, we are open books. Oscar Wilde said it well; "A man's face is his autobiography."

Our present reality is the collision point between two incredibly charged forces: our past events and choices, and our hopes and fears for the future. We meet everyone – and everyone meets us – right in the middle of our personal ground zero. The problem is while that living epicenter may register on my face, the reasons are deeply internal. Our hopes, fears, failures, and successes – our lives – are exposed through our countenances. You might not care about the particulars of my story, and I might not care about yours, but the evidence is written on our faces, nonetheless.

Here's the thing: It is hard not to react to the negatives in other people. When we encounter their tough expressions or hard eyes or miserable attitudes, we can feel affronted and take it personally.

Obviously, this is not the average Joe I meet with a scowl. They come as fast as they go. But often people are brought into our lives for a season. And rather than a snap judgment and dismissing them as irrelevant, we might ask God for His eyes to see, His heart to feel, and His mind to discern what is actually going on. God just might have sovereignly put them into our lives, where we have a role to play.

I have been praying for God to give me great consideration for the people He brings into my life. Without empathy, we are only concerned with our personal rights and inconveniences. Yes, the people we meet may act mean or foolish, but we do not know all the details of their stories.

I am not excusing people from their own responsibilities, or from the choices that have made them who they are. And I am certainly not advocating that we enable evil through misguided compassion. But realizing that I do not know all the facts about a person should restrain me from jumping to condemnation.

And we are not called only to love other people. We also need to have compassion for ourselves. How quickly we condemn ourselves as stupid or foolish, even though we know our own life story! Yet that is not how Jesus handles me at all.

How grateful I am for Jesus, Who knows my heart, knows my story, and handles me with unfailing love and compassion! His love is the answer to the quandaries in each of our lives, and to our desire to share His love with others. His love, offered through our yielded hearts, God is the only thing that can melt the hardened, soothe the hysterical, and touch the devastated.

Be honest in your judgment and do not decide at a glance (superficially and by appearances); but judge fairly and righteously.
John 7:24 AMP

You [set yourselves up to] judge according to the flesh (by what you see). [You condemn by external, human standards.] I do not [set Myself up to] judge or condemn or sentence anyone.
John 8:15 AMPC

THE SCORECARD OF ABUSE

It is fascinating how our physical bodies manifest our spiritual pain. The body is literally a scorecard keeping a record of life's events.

I knew a woman who was very stern and rarely smiled. I found out that her husband was abusive and she grew up in an alcoholic home. As she grew older, her face conformed to her attitude and bitterness.

It is not only our faces that display our life choices; the rest of the body does, as well. Muscles, digestive tissue, joints and the brain – the list goes on and on. We carry our history, and the choices we made in response to our history, in our bodies. We do not have to be physically beaten to physically bear the costs, the consequences, of painful experiences. Our bodies are affected in many ways by abuse and trauma.

For years I was an anxious man, and this stress affected my body in multiple ways. Because of this, I regularly receive massage therapy. My muscles were riddled with knots and my disks in my low back had herniated. My sin of anxiety, recorded in my body, took a toll on my physical health.

While receiving these massages, I had one therapist ask me if I had been in an accident, which I had not. The whole thing made me start to contemplate abusive scenarios and how the body registers trauma. This therapist's question was so thought provoking, I asked the Lord and waited to hear what He would say.

Psychiatry usually claims that our personalities are formed by what happens to us. I have learned from the Lord that it is often how we respond to life that solidifies our personality. Just like the body recording the scorecard of our choices, so does our personality.

While this is partially true of fallen humanity, it does not have to be for the heavenly man. Once we have been saved, we are no longer tied to life's pummeling and can even be set free from the poor choices we have made in response. The body does chronicle our life, but Christ can clear the scoreboard.

FREEDOM FROM THE POWER OF ABUSE

When we are born again, we are made new in Christ.

Therefore if anyone is in Christ, the new creation has come. The old has gone, the new is here!
2 Corinthians. 5:17 NIV

Praise God! Though the effects of our past and present environments must be processed with the Holy Spirit, those circumstances need not imprison us.

Choice is always a major factor in dealing with abuse and trauma. Choice is our power, given to us by God.

Pain, abuse, and trauma seem inevitable in this world. We all suffer from varying degrees of abuse: verbal, mental, emotional, physical, sexual…inflicted by parents, siblings, teachers, strangers, acquaintances, spouses – or even by ourselves. How unfair it would be if our past and present environments could constrain us from our future destinies in Christ!

But while our past has already happened, how we respond to our past is not set in stone. We are not limited to the prison walls of our abuse or trauma.

What we sow, we will reap. This is a spiritual and natural law. But Jesus can zero out the scorecard of sins and abuses in our bodies, whether afflicted by others or by ourselves! We born-again believers are affected by a different reality: the payment of Christ on the Cross for our sin, the forgiveness of that sin, Jesus' cleansing blood, and the power of a God Who makes all things new.

In His sovereignty, what we have seen as abuse can become

blessing!

I have read accounts of hideous abuse inflicted on children – this has happened day after day since the dawn of human history, and it continues today. The scars these children bear come from wounds caused by other human beings – who themselves were probably abused. But while we may have been powerless to prevent these tragedies, we can choose our response to what has occurred. It has been proven, we choose as early as the womb. While understanding may not be possible, our choice is intact regardless of age. Choice is every humans gift from God. No one has the power to take away that choice!

Let's look at Fanny Crosby an American mission worker, poet, lyricist, and composer, who wrote more than 8,000 hymns. What is so remarkable other than being a prolific writer and composer? She was blind from infancy due to the malpractice of a man posing as a doctor.

As an infant, Fanny Crosby contracted an eye infection. This happened while her family's physician was away so another country doctor attended the baby. This man posing as a qualified doctor treated her eyes with a hot mustard poultice. While her parent's questioned this treatment, the charlatan responded, "I am the physician and know what needs to be done!" Permanent blindness was the result of this treatment. The quack fled the town after learning the result of his treatment, which left poor Fanny blind for life.

God is either sovereign over all, or He is not sovereign at all. While this story can get our dander up for the sheer injustice, in the Hands of a sovereign God, it was a Sovereign Touch of Fanny Crosby. What seems at face value to be nothing but a tragedy, had a glorious side.

As Martha and I reflected on Fanny's life she said, "God's limitations are His gift. They bring us into our destiny. Limitations forced Fanny Crosby to become who she was." Blindness seems like a curse, but Fanny saw clearer than most and impacted the world for her Sovereign God.

Here is a poem Fanny wrote when she was only eight:

"Oh what a happy soul am I although I cannot see,
I am resolved that in this world contented I shall be.
How many blessings I enjoy that other people don't.
To weep and sigh, because I'm blind? I cannot and I won't."[1]

A mob quickly formed against Paul and Silas, and the city officials ordered them stripped and beaten with wooden rods. They were severely beaten, and then they were thrown into prison. The jailer was ordered to make sure they didn't escape. So the jailer put them into the inner dungeon and clamped their feet in the stocks. Around midnight Paul and Silas were praying and singing hymns to God, and the other prisoners were listening. Suddenly, there was a massive earthquake, and the prison was shaken to its foundations. All the doors immediately flew open, and the chains of every prisoner fell off!
Acts 16:22-26 NLT

---

1 Fanny Crosby (2008). "Fanny J. Crosby: An Autobiography", p.24, Hendrickson Publishers

Going Rigid in Trauma

I can go to human strength in response to trauma, or I can enter into my weakness with God. The Apostle Paul experienced this:

Three times I pleaded with the Lord to take [my weakness] away from me. But he said to me, "My grace is sufficient for you, for my power is made perfect in weakness"
2 Corinthians. 12:8-9 NIV

When I ignore this scriptural example, persisting in reacting to trauma or adversity in my own strength, I can reap negative physical effects. Some of these are anything but mild: irritable bowel syndrome, arthritis, autoimmune diseases, chronic fatigue, PTSD, and the like.

I am not saying that in ever case these illnesses result from resistance to God's sovereignty. But in my own life, I have seen these consequences when I have resisted God's sovereign touch rather than yielding to Him. So I wonder: How many of our wounds and physical maladies are actually a result of resistance to, rather than the infliction of, our traumas?

Think about what happens when you fall. If you stiffen your body and throw your arms forward to catch yourself, there's a higher chance of injury than if you were to not stiffen. Who among us does not naturally enter self-preserving mode?

Is it possible to go through traumatic situations with God? Can God lead us through "awful"? I believe the answer is yes.

God built this world and life so that we are dependent on

Him to survive and thrive. Our resistance to God, to the story He is writing in each of us, to the life He has given us, is what wounds us. On the other hand, when we yield to God's sovereign hand, grace enters to receive our story. This might not happen in the moment, but rather in hindsight.

How many of our physical ailments result from our resistance to God? In the past, when I have resisted God's sovereign choices for me, the result felt as if I had been beat with a bat. When I resisted my life, those choices battered me.

For instance, my being an only child. I wrestled with this fact, and tried to make my story different. The more I resisted, the more painful became the scenario. Rejection was the response because I was outside my story. Literally, friends and family with whom I tried to fill the void responded to me with rejection. And of course I tried, I was not saved, but that did not preclude me from the consequences of my choices.

Can we go through traumatic situations and remain intact? What is the difference between those who are shattered by crisis and those who emerge whole?

They continued stoning Stephen as he called on the Lord and said, "Lord Jesus, receive and accept and welcome my spirit!" Then falling on his knees [in worship], he cried out loudly, "Lord, do not hold this sin against them [do not charge them]!" When he had said this, he fell asleep [in death].
Acts 7:59-60 AMP

God is Sovereign Over Our Bodies

I remember once when a friend experienced a severe health crisis. The doctors said she had the most aggressive type of uterine cancer. She first turned to God and faced her problem through prayer. God resolved her fear and then completely healed her before starting medical treatments. A miracle on all fronts! But while hearing her painful tale, I saw something so arresting: God is completely sovereign over our bodies.

I can logic this one out all day long, but my relationship with my body is visceral and highly subjective. I have skin in the game, so to speak. After all, I am a triune being, made in the image of my Creator: I have a body, a soul, and a spirit. When my body is in bad shape, my soul can respond by addressing the issue in fear (fight or flight). This is the soul's mode of operation: scream and run, or buckle down to fix it. Either way, my *self* comes to the rescue.

My other alternative is to allow my spirit to rise up in faith that GOD will rescue me. In this scenario my spirit does not rely on logic or reason. Instead, it yields to Him in faith. It faces crises according to the facts the Father relays through the Spirit. This is opposed to basing my information on appearance. I always have this choice, but yielding to the Spirit will always be the best solution.

MOSES' LEPROUS HAND

The arresting revelation I had when hearing of my friend's health crisis was about Moses, the man chosen by God to free the Hebrew children from Egyptian slavery (See Genesis 12:1 and Exodus 1-20 to read the complete story). Approaching this particular interaction, Moses is standing ready to face down Pharaoh, Egypt's ruler, as part of God's will and plan for the Hebrews' redemption.

In this dealing, God shows Moses that He is in control of Moses' body.

Then the Lord said to Moses, "Now put your hand inside your cloak." So Moses put his hand inside his cloak, and when he took it out again, his hand was white as snow with a severe skin disease. "Now put your hand back into your cloak," the Lord said. So Moses put his hand back in, and when he took it out again, it was as healthy as the rest of his body.
Exodus 4:6-7 NLT

In essence God said to Moses, "I am sovereign over your body. I created it, I maintain it, and it is Mine!" The Lord had to show Moses this truth so He could prove He had power over Moses' world.

This is a lesson we all have to learn. God is God and God is over our bodies. Again, I can figure this out logically, but I seldom face pain or physical maladies with objectivity. In fact, I am more likely to face physical trauma in "DEFCON 1 RED ALERT" mode! Don't you?

What Moses came face-to-face with that day was his complete dependence and utter vulnerability on God. This lesson is both crucial and frightening! The fact that God is able to heal, while retaining control over whether or not He does so, scares the willies out of us.

God was not simply performing a parlor trick to entertain Moses that day like, "Watch Me pull a rabbit out of My hat!" He was putting a stake into the ground of Moses' heart: "I AM all-powerful, I AM God, and I AM in control…of even your own body!"

I, too, have come face to face with many a "leprous" situation in my life. I was helpless in the hands of a God who had power to change my situation – or not. He is able, He is willing – but He is also in control.

Moses was dependent on his God. And God proved Moses' dependence in Moses' own body, and He has done so in mine as well. It is a powerful gift to KNOW that God is sovereign over our bodies – period! If He can control our bodies, He can control our lives and our world.

Even My Body Belongs to God

"I AM over your body! Your body is under My control, not your circumstances nor your dominance, for I wield your body as MY instrument to make Myself known."

—God

I have had a love/hate relationship with my body all my life. I am grateful for its agility and capabilities, but I hate its frailty. Nothing gains my attention quicker than a health crisis. Each and every emergency feels like a life or death proposition.

Most grievous to me is feeling controlled by my body's demands. If it is required, I must respond. If a malady appears, I must face it. This glorious palace in which I live is my vehicle for life. It is both a treasure and a prison.

I have written blog posts on our website, GetAlongWithGod. com, about being my body's servant, and how that felt like a prison of servitude. I have also shared how God has used my injuries to reveal Himself in me, to shed a revelatory light of His Lordship over me, and to ignite an experience of His worship in my body.

For instance, Jesus revealed Himself to me in a totally new way after accidentally cutting my fingertip off in a juicer. Yes, that is right, I juiced my index finger on my left hand. No, it was not leprosy, but like Moses it was hugely shocking. And as with Moses, the sovereign lordship of God was firmly pronounced. "I AM all-powerful, I AM God, and I AM in control of even your body!"

What has amazed me most is this event has become very holy to me. Through this encounter, I received a revelatory light of His Lordship and an experience of His worship in my body. I will never be the same from the lessons I learn throughout this traumatic experience. The loss of my finger-tip was a small price to pay for what would come as a pay-off.

As Martha can attest, because she witnessed my whole process during this trial. I walked in a supernatural grace all the way through this situation. I drove myself to the hospital, I went through the two surgeries needed to rebuild my finger, and survived the weeks of pain and recovery with inexplicable joy and peace.

Funny thing about the whole encounter, I did not know all that the Lord had done until I was preparing to share about this experience at a conference. What happened was astonishing. Christ Himself entered into a place of deep fear in my heart so that He could worship the Father in that dark space.

During my childhood, I developed bitterness with God, mostly for not performing as I would have liked. As a result I also became a deeply fearful person. I was afraid of death in everything. Illness and injury particularly terrified me, because they all lead to death, right? Who does not feel that lump in their body and not believe it could be cancer?

My awareness of God was absent in this place of fear, and I was paralyzed in it. This area was a deep hole of darkness where Satan had the right to torment me. Where God is not enthroned, Satan has access. But God in His wonderful wisdom knew just how to address this. Christ entered my dark place of fear and explosively worshiped the Father in it. This has blown my mind! There was no worship of the Father in this area of my life and this incident with my finger gave Him entrance to fill it with His Light.

In the end, it was not comfort that I needed during this time, it was the Light of His Worship. It completely involved me, but it was not about me. The focus was not my finger, it was worship of the Father. In my opinion I would have directed God to get me out of pain and heal me quickly, but what transpired was the bursting forth of the Son's worship of the Father in my dark place. Humanly this is so counterintuitive, but it has changed my entire perspective.

EXPLOSIVE WORSHIP

Because of that experience, we have even greater confidence in the message proclaimed by the prophets. You must pay close attention to what they wrote, for their words are like a lamp shining in a dark place — until the Day dawns, and Christ the Morning Star shines in your hearts.
2 Peter 1:19 NLT

This is exactly what happened during my finger episode — Within my dismal and squalid place, Christ, the Morning Star, rose in my heart.

Christ rose up in my heart to bring forth worship where no worship was present. He entered my squalid place of fear and torment with the Light of His own worship for the Father. Imagine, Christ Himself came into my heart to be the worship where I was bound and unable to worship.

This worship was not for me nor was it about me, but it completely included me. I experienced Christ's own union with and adoration of His Father within my frame.

I pray that they will all be one, just as You and I are one — as You are in Me, Father, and I am in You. And may they be in Us so that

> *the world will believe You sent Me. I have given them the glory*
> *You gave Me, so they may be one as We are one. I am in them*
> *and You are in Me. May they experience such perfect unity that*
> *the world will know that You sent Me and that You love them as*
> *much as You love Me.*
> *John 17:21-23 NLT*

This was a pivot in my whole concept of worship and a dynamic turning point in my life. I was not lying in bed with my injured finger, singing songs and hymns. Externally I was laying there in a bed for weeks with a mitt on my hand. You would not have known any difference. But in the spiritual I was being indwelt by the Son of God, who worshiped His Father in me.

After hearing of Christ's worship in my heart, a lovely lady asked, "What did it look like?" Oh, how refreshing that was! It was not sympathy for God taking me on a painful path; instead, it was the child-like wonder of a fascinated heart: "Tell me!"

I do not remember how exactly I answered her, but I can say that the worship was explosive. It was loud and big and exuberant. It was far beyond me singing with my eyes closed and hands raised. Christ's worship in me was beyond anything I had even seen or known as worship. It was complete, total, unrelenting focus, with passion and power beyond anything I could humanly muster. The Father and Son were ONE in me! Talk about a Sovereign Touch!

It completely convinced me of what the Lord said to me, "I am over your body!"

The Lord of Adversity

Our Lord is the Lord of all adversity. At certain points in my walk I thought that my adversities were obstacles in the way of my pursuit of God. I thought they were hurdles that I needed to overcome – impediments to my walk – that would prevent me from reaching the destiny God had for me.

But now I ask: Could these obstacles be in place to shepherd me? Could God have used adversity to direct and guide me towards Himself?

Suppose you were born into a family of avid sportsmen, but you had not one stitch of athleticism in your body. Maybe baseball was your family's drug of choice, but you had an arm that was weak and malformed, either from birth, or through an accident. Either way, your deformity caused you tremendous shame and heartache because you just could not compete with – or even play alongside – your family. You cursed and struggled with what you were unable to do, and you wilted under a weight of scorn.

Could God be sovereign over this adversity? Could God have purposed your inborn limitation to prevent you from pursuing sports? Could this limitation that caused you such shame be God's own jealousy for you and your attention? Could He be saving you from an idolatry that would have led you away from Him forever?

Here is another example: Imagine that your biological parents did not want children, and when they discovered you were on the way, they decided that you would ruin their life plans. So they put you up for adoption.

Even though you were adopted into a healthy home, a

feeling of rejection seemed to dog every relationship in your life. You found yourself always waiting for the other shoe to drop, for someone else to reject you, too.

How in the world, you ask, could such a lifelong fear of rejection come at the hand of God?

But just think: What if God was saving you from biological parents who, in their own narcissism, would have destroyed you? Might their presence in your life have prevented your salvation? Does your fear of rejection make you just needy enough to look toward an Eternal Father for love and rescue?

These examples are hypothetical: You can fill in the blanks with your own adversity. Is it a physical malady? A generational curse that has plagued your whole life? A heart attitude from which you just cannot escape?

Yes, you and I are accountable for our own sins, and most of us, at some time or another, sin in the way we deal with our adversities. But what if the original scenario you are dealing with was set in place to humble you and make you completely dependent on God? Is God able to exert His sovereignty even over the direction of my own fallen nature?

Yes, I believe that His sovereignty is beyond even my weakness, be it physical, mental, emotional or moral. He is either God of all, or He is not God at all! Christ is the Lord of all our adversity, no matter what that adversity might be.

Like you, I see things about myself that I would have preferred to change. For example, naturally I was an independent and bold child. I would have done or tried anything but as I aged, I developed an inordinate fear of death. I believe

God used that fear to hem me in until I was ready to come to Him. The fear was debilitating, even crippling at times, but it was a "keeping factor": God in His sovereignty used it to constrain me, to keep me until I was ready to become His child.

THE PROBLEM OF EVIL

Please hear me clearly: I am NOT saying that God is the author of evil. He cannot be, but He is the owner of the book of the history of man and of our lives.

This truly is our dilemma! How can we say that God in His sovereignty used something that seems bad to us in His plan for us? Did He, then, create those bad situations, circumstances, etc.?

In their book, *Who Made God? And Answers to Over 100 Other Tough Questions of Faith*, general editors Ravi Zacharias and Norman Geisler address the origin of evil. They note that God could have created us as robots, without the free will that makes evil possible. But God did not want robots: He wanted humans made in His image, and free will is part of His image. He wanted humans who could choose freely to love Him. The editors quote apologist Paul Little as saying, "God apparently thought it worth the risk of creating us as we are."[2]

Someone has said, "Evil is the absence of God." When Adam and Eve chose to disobey God's clear instructions in the Garden of Eden, they chose to take God out of – to absent

---

2 Little, Paul, Know Why You Believe, p. 81. Quoted in *Who Made God: And Answers to Over 100 Other Tough Questions of Faith*. General Editors: Ravi Zacharias and Norman Geisler. Zondervan, Grand Rapids, MI, C. 2003, p.36

God – from the equation of their action. I agree that when we choose to dismiss God from our lives, we invite evil to be present. Evil is the result of decided to be masters of our own fate, instead of submissive to God's best for us.

I am in awe of God's control, ultimately even of my willful decisions. I belong to God and I am His to maneuver in whatever way He chooses. God being absolutely sovereign makes me understand the seemingly inscrutable Scripture that calls us to thank Him for everything:

*No matter what happens, always be thankful, for this is God's will
for you who belong to Christ Jesus.*
1 Thessalonians 5:18 TLB

Life Has Hurt You

Even when we think we understand, at least with our heads, that God did not create evil, we still ask: If God is the owner of the Book of all of life, why did He allow pain in my story? Why did He not prevent things from hurting me so deeply? And if God did allow painful situations to happen in my life, then how am I to trust Him now?

Though none of us is entitled to know "Why?" our Father God often tells us. I have asked Him many "Why?" questions, and He has often lovingly and kindly obliged me with answers.

However, knowing the purpose of an event or circumstance in our lives does not alleviate the emotional pain of its happening. Knowing the "Why?" may satisfy our mind, but bruised feelings dwell in the heart. And only in the heart can our demand for satisfaction be met.

I have learned that our demand for answers is never satisfied until we surrender to His sovereignty over our pain. Bitterness with life demands an answer, posing as God. But the Most High will never surrender His throne, and the pride of bitterness refuses His Lordship, requiring His exit.

When we bow to His Lordship over our difficulties, something happens in our hearts. God, unmoved by our demand to *be* God, to pridefully have things *our* way, is moved by our pain and our willingness to yield to Him.

No one is exempt from painful life occurrences. I do not know the pain you bear, just as no one but God knows mine. I might not be able to fathom enduring what you have endured. What might crush you might not faze me, and vice versa.

But our Father knows all. And He longs to give us peace under His sovereign care. Yes, He often uses situations and circumstances to wound us so that we will seek Him, instead of depending on ourselves. But His desire is to father us, with tender loving care, through the ups and downs of the events that shape our lives.

We may never understand the purpose of certain life happenings on this side of eternity, but God calls us to Himself to give us the grace to walk through them. When we persist in demanding satisfactory answers to our "Whys?" we force ourselves to carry a heavy weight. And understanding "Why?" may not lift the pain anyway.

PAIN AND BITTERNESS

I know that the words I am about to write will burn as they rub against any bitterness you may be carrying, as they have for me. But I need to write them: *Only faith and surrender accepts God's sovereignty.*

What kind of faith am I talking about? Faith that God is God, and that His character is impeccable. Faith that God is love, even as we suffer terrible pain. Faith that He is holy, even as our troubles seem to overwhelm us. Faith that His Will and purpose for us and for this world are perfect, no matter how much I want to scream my objections.

When our hands and hearts are motivated by bitterness, they become like claws – claws that pinch and harm everyone around us. Claws that latch on insistently, demanding explanations – and finding none.

Rather than demanding, a heart postured to surrender will yield to God, and opens to receive His embrace. A heart of surrender calls out for – and receives – God's mercy. The painful situation may not end, but God gives grace and acceptance to endure.

God receives His children as a Father. He can be trusted with our pain. He can bring eternal reward out of every difficult circumstance; one day He will wipe away every tear from our eyes. He is sovereign over us all, the Worker of miracles. Out of what we see as pointless pain, He can form destiny and eternity. He is the Master Craftsman, the Forger from Fire, our Beloved, the One who ever works toward the High Purpose He plans for us, and for our world.

He is not afraid of our railings. He does not shrink from our accusations. But when we get still before Him, and relinquish our raised fists and stubborn demands, He meets us with kindness, everlasting friendship, and overwhelming grace.

Making your ear attentive to wisdom and inclining your heart to understanding; yes, if you call out for insight and raise your voice for understanding, if you seek it like silver and search for it as for hidden treasures, then you will understand the fear of the Lord and find the knowledge of God.
Proverbs 2:2-5 ESV

Forgiveness and Sovereignty

As I prayed for this book, I kept hearing the Lord say, "There is no forgiveness without sovereignty." What could He mean by this statement? Personal forgiveness is never fully resolved until sovereignty covers it. This is huge: God's sovereignty and our forgiveness are inseparable!

When I first came to Shulamite Ministries, the Lord asked me to enter into a season of solitude. He said, "Come away with Me." So I did. Jesus wanted to unplug me from a life of effort, fear, and hysteria. I had spent many years reaping the consequences of bitterness and He was calling me out of that treadmill to hear Him. A season of separateness was how He chose to do it.

Over the two-year period that followed, Jesus allowed me to try Him for all of my offenses with Him, to hurl at Him all of my "Whys?"

"Why did this happen?"
"Why didn't You prevent this?"
"What was this for?"
"Why did You allow this?"

This process did not take place with pretty worship music playing in the background. I was not disrespectful, but I was raw and I was real with God. I found out that He was up for the challenge. And as God allowed me to dialog with Him I was amazed that He was willing to answer me. My inquiry did not upset His sovereignty or His right to do as He willed. He did not crush me for daring to be bold with Him, the Creator of the Universe. He was truly interested in my heart, wanting it to be His completely, even with all my ugliness and offenses.

FORGIVENESS OF OUR DEEPEST WOUNDS

One of the things God used to open me up during my season of solitude was Martha Kilpatrick's book *All and Only*.[3] Through its pages, God showed me His sovereign hand over everything. He showed me how He uses this life with all its hurts to mold and knead us into the persons He longs for us to be. And the most effective tool for this purpose is our offenses.

Why? Because offenses are rooted in our hearts. Little offenses that can be shrugged off are one thing, but the arrows that truly wound us come from our closest relationships: relationships with our father, mother, sister, brother, pastor, spouse. These arrows access our hearts deeply, often wounding us for a lifetime.

Jesus said, "Blessed are those who are not offended in Me" (Matthew 11:6). And if He is truly sovereign, then it follows that all of these offenses we experience are in Him.

In the "Big Ten," God commands us: "Honor your father and mother" (Exodus 20:12). It is important for us to recognize that our Heavenly Father uses our earthly fathers and mothers to shape our lives, regardless of what they did to us.

Some people experience heinous offenses and abuse at the hands of others. And I would never personally ask someone to forgive these heinous offenses: It is not mine to do, nor would I presume. In fact, as I see and hear of their pain, I cry, "Dear Jesus, have mercy, that's horrible!" But I realize that in

---

3 Kilpatrick, Martha, All and Only: The First Word and the Last, Shulamite Ministries INC. 1998

sovereignty, He was at work in and through these offenses. And I discovered the following principle:

We have to make peace and deal with the sovereignty of God in order to forgive.

Let me repeat what the Lord told me: "There is no forgiveness without sovereignty." There is no way we can truly forgive unless we are willing to accept God's sovereignty and receive His goodness in all that happened, including our offenses. It is simply impossible.

After my season of solitude and my trying of the Lord, I concluded that I do not want to serve a God who is not fully in control. Though I am completely vulnerable to Him when I hold this belief, I am also safer than I could ever be otherwise. He gives me His grace to live through anything He might sovereignly bring into my existence. And my acceptance of His sovereign touch gives me the ability to see beyond the circumstances, and to gaze into His glorious face.

God does not shy away from the things that might cause me pain. He perfectly uses them to bring me to Himself.

I can only truly know God as I embrace Him as my Sovereign.

The Healing Balm of Sovereignty

We can't escape God's supreme rule and Lordship. At first glance this irrefutable wall of God's sovereignty can be daunting. But there is a softer side to sovereignty that many fail to experience. Accepting God's sovereignty gives us the grace to accept *life*.

When finally facing the terrible repercussions of sins done towards us as well as our own sins, we could easily drown in a pool of despair. How can we live with what has been done or what we've done? How could we possibly atone? God's sovereignty can be a tremendous source of comfort and solace in this dark moment. His sovereign touch gives us the grace to be able to face and accept our faults and sins, especially where others were hurt.

For the truly repentant man, sovereignty becomes a balm of healing. God comes in to heal and relieve me of the overwhelming burden. What is too much for me to face alone, the blood of Christ and His sovereign plan cover with grace.

I am not saying that we are entitled to a "Get out of jail free" card. I do not get to abuse others and then say, "Why are you so upset? It was God's sovereign plan for you." That's repulsive! I am speaking of a powerful work of grace offered to the one who has sunk deep below the waves of repentance.

Sovereignty does not absolve me of guilt or responsibility. I will answer for all my evil responses, every idle word I spoke, and my wicked deeds. The consequence of my sins will still come upon me, for I reap what I have sown. But even beyond the work of repentance, recompense, and forgiveness, there is the healing of sovereignty.

God transcends the evil we all do. He does this because He is sovereign and our Father. The sins of the parent done to the child will become God's sovereign work in that child's life. We all have to bow to His Lordship. The sinner and sinned-upon alike have to deal with the God who is sovereign.

Healing comes when we know that God is God and able to transcend our sins and the sins done against us. Though I am accountable to God, His sovereign hand offers me grace to be able to face another day. Sovereignty is the satisfaction of resting in His omnipotent plan, knowing that the blood of Jesus cleanses. God's sovereignty tells me that He knows the plans He has for me, so now I can take a step from despair. God IS God!

I thank God for this grace! I praise Him for His sovereign touch. And I am so grateful to know that nothing I have done in my life is beyond my sovereign God's reach. He will come for those I have wounded as He has come for me. I love His sovereign gift of grace.

As for you, you meant evil against me, but God meant it for good
in order to bring about this present result, to preserve many people
alive.
Genesis 50:20 NASB

Is This for God's Good or Mine Too?

To the one who delights in the sovereignty of God the clouds not only have a 'silver lining' but they are silver all through, the darkness only serving to offset the light.

Arthur W. Pink
English Bible Teacher
1886 - 1952

And we know that for those who love God all things work together for good, for those who are called according to His purpose.
Romans 8:28 ESV

Witness of God's Perfection

Many teenagers believe they are smarter than their parents. When we gain a little knowledge, we view ourselves as greater than those who raised us. I wish this attitude ended with our teen years, but unfortunately many of us hold this stance for a lifetime.

It is not that different in our relationship with God. All too often we come to Him thinking we know better than He does. We believe He is slow, possibly neglectful or (yikes!) stupid. We may even think, "God is not the best judge of my well-being." We usually don't verbalize these thoughts, but God sees the attitudes of our hearts. Self-preservation is a strong, rebellious root!

In light of this sinful tendency, I want to celebrate the Lord's perfecting and perfection. It is so completely different from our human perfectionism. Why?

I do not know if I am gaining wisdom with age, or if the fear of God (reverence, awe and respect) has increased exponentially in my spirit, but I keep seeing God's perfect hand in the lives of many believers around me. Yes, individual happenings may disturb me or make me fearful for them, but seen through His view it can be beautiful. Observing how the Father works circumstances together like the weaving of a tapestry lets me see just how masterful He is. It has been my privilege to see God's plan play out over the span of their lives. I love it!

In my past, there were times that I certainly thought I knew better that God. I was raised as a Florida city boy but God brought me to the mountains of North Georgia. While I loved the beauty of the mountains, I really preferred the convenience of a city. God tricked me! Not only did the Lord bring me to the mountains, He revealed them to me as perfect for me. I was designed with a heart that flourishes in a mountain-scape. Gardening, shepherd of sheep and goats, and the slower pace... I discovered was perfect.

PAIN IN PERFECTION

God, in His amazing Fatherhood, leads us into His own perfecting of us and His perfection of our lives. He weaves together seemingly negative situations with seemingly positive circumstances in order to raise and shepherd His beloved children.

I say "seemingly" because in truth, we really do not know which circumstances are positive and negative. If only we could live in the faith that our Abba Father – our loving Daddy – is quite different from our earthly role models. If only we could release ourselves into His hands, allowing Him to guide and lead us. If only we could allow Him to define every situation in our lives by His thoughts, rather than filtering them through our flawed, human opinions and feelings. Yet even in our frailty, He will orchestrate the steps of those who love Him.

It may not seem like it in the moment, but perspective and outcomes reveal that He is able to work all things together for the good of those who love Him (Romans 8:28).

God, however, does not always put as high a premium on painless living as we do. The absence of our pain is not His goal. His motivation has His ultimate goals in mind, whereas our motivations are limited by our present moment's discomfort. Comfort is an unsatisfied mistress: comfort and ease always demand complete satisfaction regardless of the consequences. But our God will always reap the greatest of rewards from all events and circumstances, no matter how we see them from our limited perspective.

The Lord is the grand orchestrator of all things. He always moves to bring forth His plans and goals. I am enamored with His craftsmanship in using circumstances and situations to grow us in His character and image.

One of His most amazing works is to intricately weave together multiple lives, in concert, to bring about the beauty of His children's growth, freedom, and increase in the knowledge of His own beautiful Person. It is a lot easier to gain a "bird's eye view" of someone else's life, as an observer, than it is to be in the thick of your own battle. It takes much more time and faith to see God's intricate, Sovereign Touch in our own lives rather than just witnessing it in another's.

I have learned one thing by observing God's handiwork in other's lives. By listening to the Father I can have the privilege to stand in faith for God's perfecting of another's life. In faith, I can believe for His definition of a circumstance. Planting our feet in faith—in the reality of His Fathering— can assist someone else to break through his or her circumstances to see that Fathering.

Remember, it is much easier to remain faithful to God when we are not in the midst of trial and tribulation, so we must depend on the Spirit to give us sensitivity to those who are hurting. But we can be His servants to strengthen another's walk.

I certainly know that God has used His people to accomplish such a ministry of presence and vision for me! Incredible power is bestowed on me when a brother or sister helps me to catch the unwavering vision that God is good, that He is God, and that He is currently doing a good work in my life despite all appearances. Sometimes this is just the sanity we need to help us survive one more day.

"My thoughts are nothing like your thoughts," says the Lord. "And My ways are far beyond anything you could imagine. For just as the heavens are higher than the earth, so My ways are higher than your ways and My thoughts higher than your thoughts. Isaiah 55:8-9 NLT

I think a Arthur Pink quote works best here:

"To the one who delights in the sovereignty of God the clouds not only have a 'silver lining' but they are silver all through, the darkness only serving to offset the light."
Arthur W. Pink
English Bible Teacher, 1886-1952

A Life Designed for Knowing God

Our life events and situations have one purpose in their design: that we would come to know our God. Happiness in itself is not the goal but rather the result of connecting with God. Life is a continual invitation by our Creator for us to know Him in every facet of existence. And knowing Him is the source of our fulfillment and joy.

This knowledge of God is not mere head knowledge. It is an experiential, interactive and intimate knowing. It is yada, which in Hebrew means "an increasingly deep intimacy." It is "knowing" as in the caress of bridal communion. Imagine! Life is the stage set for our intimate knowledge of God, a rich knowing of the Most High. All of life (what we see as good and bad) is a continual invitation to know our Creator in every facet of existence. And knowing Him is the source of our fulfillment and joy.

Every situation undergoes a transformation from a "chance happening" to be enjoyed or endured into an opportunity to know God. This is not just a Pollyanna-like view of life: It is the purpose and design of life for those called by God.

In the past I have approached unpleasant or traumatic situations as obstacles to get over or move past. I know in my life, this involved paying therapists to free me from those occurrences in my life that I wish to forget. To help me to refocus and leave behind what has caused me pain. And, if it is not possible to talk it out, maybe a doctor will medicate it out of me.

In saying this I am not discounting the necessity for therapy or medication for those of us who need it. I am simply trying to demonstrate a higher view of the whole.

Martha Kilpatrick's booklet *God's Sovereignty*, contains a powerful illustration of this concept:

"You are a book, 'a living epistle known and read of men' (2 Corinthians 3:3). God has written a story on you. He has a message through you – you will be healthy and sane only as you live that story, deliver your message and not another, because any other will be a lie. We are capable of making up our own story!"[1]

I can expend my energies trying to get free from life, or I can seek God's overarching intent for my pain, and it's given purpose. Pain with purpose is easier to endure than pointless agony.

Life, in all its multifaceted expressions, is intended to grow in us the intimate knowledge of our great God. Is it painless or easy? No! But within this world-view, hopelessness becomes hope, and the painful becomes purposed.

[For my determined purpose is] that I may know Him [that I may progressively become more deeply and intimately acquainted with Him, perceiving and recognizing and understanding the wonders of His Person more strongly and more clearly], and that I may in that same way come to know the power outflowing from His resurrection [which it exerts over believers], and that I may so share His sufferings as to be continually transformed [in spirit into His likeness even] to His death, [in the hope]
Philippians 3:10 AMPC

---

1 Kilpatrick, Martha, *God's Sovereignty*, "Cause and Effect." Shulamite Ministries INC, Copyright 1986, 2009, pg. 21.

Grappling with God's Sovereignty

My parents prided themselves on raising me to be an independent individual. At times, this rearing style felt to me neglectful, but what I have learned is that it was all perfectly orchestrated for me, personally. God's tailor-made design of my life, God's choice for how I would be parented, planted me in an environment in which I could thrive in my circumstances.

The reality is that I was not neglected at all; I was completely cared for, with every provision I needed.

As I reflect on my upbringing, I realize that it was not what happened to me that hurt me – it was my resistance to what happened to me that wreaked havoc in my life. We all have the grace to go through all that God allows. This may seem like a bitter pill at times, but also a sweet reality. Life may wound us, but our rigid resistance to that wounding is more detrimental than the wounding itself.

Having said that, we have to look at the worst-case scenario: What about the severely abused? You and I could each recite a list of abuses that are currently being experienced, cruelties which cause the skin of even the most-hardened of us to crawl.

Still, all that I have said about God's sovereignty and His grace remains true. God is sovereign, and He will give us grace for the life He has asked us to live. Whether we can always discern it or not, our personal world is set up for us to experience God. I do not say this coldly, or dispassionately. I say it with fear and trembling.

Am I – or are you – supposed to lie down and deliberately

allow ourselves to be abused? Of course not! But in God's eyes, our lives and the things that happen to us in the course of our lives all point toward one goal: that we would know the One who created us.

Note: The goal is not our happiness. It is for us to see God and recognize our need for Him. Ultimately our lives are preparation for eternity. We are to become increasingly acquainted with Jesus. It is for His purpose that we are here.

Gazing at our life circumstances, we need to understand that nothing happens by chance. What a comfort to know that God holds the whole world in His hands. As we grasp this truth, His sovereignty becomes more hopeful than frightening. Even though I may not like how circumstances, situations or relationships affect my life, God's character and goodness are set as a seal on each one to achieve the perfection He is orchestrating.

God's Amazing Hand of Providence

God has the ability to move the man or woman who is surrendered to living in His Will. God can maneuver a person into exactly the most optimal position for following His Will. Theologically this is called "the Hand of Providence." At its core, "providence" is God enacting His guidance on His creation.

This is such good news! God is above all and works all things together for His good pleasure. Hallelujah! His pleasure is always good, and means good for us!

John Nelson Darby, an Anglo-Irish Bible teacher in the 1800's wrote, "God's ways are behind the scenes; but He moves all of the scenes He is behind."[2] Wonderful, right? We see this clearly in the biblical Book of Esther, which details the story of God's miraculous deliverance of the Jews from certain annihilation. God's name is never mentioned anywhere in this book of the Bible, but His movement, His Hand, His actions, are seen all over it.

If we but look, we will see God's fingerprint everywhere, the evidence of His moving Hand. This is His providence.

Skip Heitzig, founder and current senior pastor of Calvary of Albuquerque said, "God strings together ordinary events, places, and people so that they align perfectly with His will, His ultimate plan."[3] We do not have a weak, insipid God, but One who is able and is truly involved in human history,

---

2 H. H. Snell., G. V. Wilgram, Edward Dennett, H. C. Anstey, C. H. Mackintosh (2015). "The Christian's Friend and Instructor: Christian Magazine Volume 16, 1889 Edition", p.70, Irving Risch
3 "Bloodline: Tracing God's Rescue Plan from Eden to Eternity", p. 81 Harvest House Publishers (2019)

and in our individual lives. The Shepherd of our hearts is the Shepherd of our lives, as well.

Do we see God's providence only in the lives of His children who are utterly surrendered to His Will? If we look, we will see God's providence everywhere. But the man or woman who is yielded to being IN God's Will benefits the most from God's providence, because he or she experiences Jesus Himself, as well as the joy and adventure of living under His Shepherding care.

I know this personally. I could relate to you many instances in my own life where I knew God was working, even though I was not at all living as His child. I did not particularly enjoy the adventure of His navigation, but I did reap the benefits.

One such occasion happened when I was in my late teens. I was in major rebellion and resistance to God and my parents. My path was full of drinking, drugs, and rabble-rousing. I was filled with bitterness as well as depression. I was a rebel, but that independence did not make me happy.

One night a group of us went out to a three phase power tower (you know, the large ones that carry electric power from the station to distant communities). Well, some of us had the smart idea to climb up to the top of it. I was not one of the daredevils, but I was certainly a witnessing participant.

Up they went, higher and higher, until finally, the police arrived and told us we had to leave the field, we were trespassing. One of the guys even fell and busted up his face. The police did not care, we had to leave the area, NOW!

As we shuffled out of the field and into a trailer park, I heard the Lord say, "You don't deserve this, but go to this dark single-wide trailer and knock on the door and ask them to call you a cab." I just obediently followed. I knew that Voice.

I grabbed one of my friends and proceeded to the door. It felt so weird, but I knocked. After a few moments, the door opened revealing a naked man who demanded an answer, "WHAT?" I told him we were lost and could he call us a cab. He agreed and slammed the door in our face.

I did not know if this gentleman was going to call the cops or a cab, but we sat on the stoop and waited. After about twenty minutes a cab arrived and we proceeded to get in and start to drive way. While pulling out of the driveway, we saw up ahead a number of police cars with their lights flashing. As we drove by I realized the people we were with were all being arrested. They each went to jail that night, while me and my friend rode away in a taxi.

How? It was not that I escaped that consequences of my sin, I just received the Father's grace that night. This was one of many situations God used to airlift me out of my sinful life. God always gets His man, and eventually He got me!

The Hand of Providence is sovereign control and amazing grace wrapped into one package. While we may make our own plans, it is God who determines, establishes, and directs our steps
Proverbs 16:9

Who is Behind My Distractions?

Life is full of distractions and diversions. We were never promised a path of no resistance. In fact, we are guaranteed quite the opposite. But what is the source of our obstacles? Could these detours actually be divine in nature?

In the past, I usually considered distractions to be kicks of the enemy rather than taps from the Lord. When I planned for things to happen according to my schedule and by my time frame, I have to confess, I felt justified in blaming the obstacles and obstructions on the enemy of our souls. It was easy to say, "Just stop it, devil," when things did not happen as I planned. My response was more often anger than gratitude.

Recently, however, I was speaking to a friend about a trial he was experiencing. He was laid off of his job with no prospects of employment due to the misdeeds of others. Unexpectedly, I saw his obstacle in a different light; as God's Sovereign Touch on his life, leading him in a different direction, toward a destiny of which he had never even dreamed. His path was to take a turn where he would actually be pushed into a position he had been trained for all his life. The loss of his job was an advancement of his calling.

Why was I so surprised? Could our distractions be more about God's love and leading than about Satan's trying to run us into a ditch? Could they be a tap on the shoulder from the Lord to say, "Hey, come over here; I need some face time!" This realization would certainly cause us to view distractions with less resistance. And because we are His children, does He not have the right to divert our steps?

If God is sovereign, and we are abiding in Him (see John

The Sovereign Touch

15), then all of the bumps in our roads are under His control. Even if the enemy claims to be their source, the reality is that even our distractions can serve God's purpose. If God is sovereign, then nothing escapes His grasp, knowing, and control. Even my distractions can reveal His heart of love and sovereign touch.

Here is a caution, however: Sometimes we fight distractions furiously, saying, "I have to get this task done NOW, God!" This attitude may expose our true desire to be in control. Is my agenda more important than His timing, His will, and our relationship? Ouch! This is such a check on my heart!

I want to live in God's hands. I want to live surrendered to His path. And I want to live hearing His tender whispers that beckon my gaze and my time.

It is easy to get caught up in my "much to do about nothing" moments. I can spin the wheels of "my agenda" while losing the point of life – Jesus Himself!

I have a long relationship with doing. And I come from a long line of doers. But if my incessant activities arise out of my plan for my life, they are leading me away from Jesus, not to Him.

Uphold my steps in Your paths, That my footsteps may not slip.
Psalm 17:5 NKJV

Is Sovereignty All About Control?

Absolute sovereignty is what I love to ascribe to God. God's sovereignty has ever appeared to me, a part of His glory. It has often been my delight to approach God and adore Him as a sovereign God.

Jonathan Edwards
Widely acknowledged to be America's most important and
original philosophical theologian
1703 – 1758

In Him we have obtained an inheritance, having been pre-destined according to the purpose of Him who works all things according to the counsel of His will . . .
Ephesians 1:11 NKJV

But I've Been Wronged!

In this section I want to run through some examples of God's sovereign hand moving through dealings I have had with others. Each has become a living parable to show me the sovereignty of God everywhere. Again I say, God is either sovereign over all, or He is not sovereign at all.

WHY HAVE I BEEN WRONGED?

For many years, every web development team that Shulamite Ministries contracted repeatedly wronged us. From the initial updates to a full Web 2.0 redesign, all the way through to our present needs, we were mistreated. Promises were made, promises were paid for, and then those promises were broken. From begging website developers to fulfill their commitments to dealing with businesses that just outright reneged on their obligations. Nonetheless, these firms went to the bank with our money...smiling. It has been a major source of frustration for me as well as a huge time vacuum. So why were we wronged?

God is always interested in the heart of a man. Bits of data and bytes of memory have as much importance to Him as pieces of paper promising monetary value. Though I can get completely worked up with injustices and broken promises, He does not seem as disturbed as me. Why, God, were we cheated?

Here's the answer: Who is God? If I look to man to do what's right, I will be sorely disappointed. And why is the sting so great? Because it is idolatry. Man has never been, nor will he ever be, my Source. I cannot, nor can any man, defend my rights—I have none. Scampering about maintaining my rights, like a squirrel socking away nuts, is foolish. It is also foolhardy to think that any man is going to do right by me. I have no rights that God Himself does not maintain. At the end of the day, God is my Source, there is no other.

So does this mean I'm supposed to just lie down like a red carpet rolled out for the world to trample on? No! I must first and foremost look to God to be my rights. He is my mediator, and an apt one at that. He is able to do more in a moment than I can do with months or years of struggle and work. But in order to have this work, I must yield my rights to Him. He then becomes my rights. When His Will is my rights, then I have peace. This is very difficult to reconcile with the statement "But I've been wronged!" echoing through my heart.

What if most of my frustrations have been my pushing against God's own hand? Is He looking for my face to turn towards Him rather than man and myself? Are these frustrations merely invitations to bring Him in to my difficulties? And what is the outcome of His involvement over my fleshly bulldozing?

Often I have gone to God and just railed about my situation. I was not trying to be clean and prettied up; I was exposing my heart to Him. In this case I was raw and angry over a company that stole money from the ministry. I had called American Express and they could do nothing; the purchase was past the 60-day dispute window. The web firm said they refused to do anything. They had our money but they no longer offered the service... "So sorry." I had been fighting this fight for months and nothing had changed — except my blood pressure.

After my railing to God in honesty and transparency, I felt He led me to call yet again. I spoke calmly and straightforwardly. They refunded our money. So did God just want to be the Source of my entire focus? Could I have avoided all the heartache? Probably not. We learn lessons in the fire, not simply by the principle.

Does this mean if I go to God, He will be a bully on my behalf? Will I get my way? Will He be my grand enforcer? No! My surrender, my following, my yielding to His Will is always the work on the table. He might have just as easily said, "Let it all go." Sovereignty is a huge pill to take, but the fruitless expending of my efforts is a poisonous dose that kills my joy and life. Bowing to His Will as my rights leads to peace and fellowship with my God.

My Enemies Only Devour My Flesh

My enemies and my painful situations in life cannot claim my spirit; they are only allowed to devour my flesh. As long as I remain open-faced towards God and thank Him for everything, bitterness cannot retake my soul. This turns out to be a service to me. God uses my enemies and difficulties to destroy that which separates me from Him.

Remember how the enemies of Israel were often used to scourge the flesh and sin from Israel's midst? Yet once the purifying work had taken place, then the enemies themselves were vanquished. In the same way, my enemies are used to prune that which stands opposed to my deep relationship and union with God. God can use whatever He wishes to accomplish this: circumstances, situations, and yes, my enemies as well. Doesn't this make you want to celebrate God's sovereign hand in your life?

The Lord is my light and my salvation — whom should I fear? The Lord is the stronghold of my life — of whom should I be afraid? When evildoers came against me to devour my flesh, my foes and my enemies stumbled and fell. Though an army deploys against me, my heart is not afraid; though a war breaks out against me, still I am confident. I have asked one thing from the Lord; it is what I desire: to dwell in the house of the Lord all the days of my life, gazing on the beauty of the Lord and seeking Him in His temple. For He will conceal me in His shelter in the day of adversity; He will hide me under the cover of His tent; He will set me high on a rock.
Psalm 27:1-5 HCSB

Christ's enemies had nothing in Him to devour. And when I am in Him, my enemies find nothing to devour in me either. It is only the dead branches of my sinful human nature on which God allows them to snack. Again, it is a service to me.

Not that I am running around recruiting enemies or looking for difficult situations, but when they come – as they inevitably will – they come to benefit me. "You meant evil against me, but God meant it for good" (Genesis 50:20). When I am in Christ, everything is for my good.

Jesus says, "Simon, Simon, Satan has asked to sift you as wheat.
But I have prayed for you, Simon, that your faith may not fail.
And when you have turned back, strengthen your brothers."
Luke 22:31-32 HCSB

The enemy is not given free rein to ravage me. He must ask God first! I know this part of sovereignty makes us squirm but it is true nonetheless. The devil is not all-powerful or all-knowing. He is still but a servant under God's control. He must ask permission to try and to tempt us, so if we are being assailed, it is in God's hands and is for our benefit. To live in rebellion is to serve Satan my life on a silver platter, but if I am God's in Christ, my enemies can do no real harm to me.

I am thinking of a situation a few years back when we had a major enemy with a desire to destroy us. This individual's attacks were deeply personal, utterly vicious, and totally malicious. They outright lied and slandered us to another ministry, which unfortunately severed the relationship with that ministry. He would not be corrected about hurting someone. It was revenge. My response to Martha was, "They're just paying our price." What I meant is that people are either the Bride of Christ or the tools used to prepare her. If you have an enemy and belong to God, then He is using them to make you ready.

"All right, you may test him," the Lord said to Satan. "Do what-
ever you want with everything he possesses, but don't harm him
physically." So Satan left the Lord's presence.
Job 1:12 NLT

I am not saying that there is joy in having enemies or walking through painful situations. Pruning is still surgical cutting, even if the target is dead wood. But with Bridal preparation on the table, it makes the attacks more palatable. I am
here, after all, for the single purpose of my preparation to
be the Bride of Christ. All will serve the Lord in His eternal
purpose, even those whom we call enemy.

When you have a mandate from the God of heaven, God will
see that your commission is fulfilled – your enemies will not
prevail against you. If you are put out of one place God will
open other doors….A committee, or board, or synod may
turn you out of every church on earth but they cannot turn
you out of the Church of heaven, for the heavens do rule.[1]

---

1 T. Austin-Sparks, British pastor, speaker, author, 1888-1971.

Sovereignty in the Microcosm

God is sovereign over ALL,
within things both big and small.

Let's look at God's sovereignty in the minuscule and seemingly insignificant scenarios. It is here where the treasures are deeply meaningful because they are usually unexpected. In these seemingly unimportant circumstances we find enjoyment between God and us alone.

I go to the pool in a neighboring town three or four times a week to swim. I enjoy the forty-five minute drive to and from the gym, and I enjoy my time in the water. Quite often the Lord gives me ideas and inspiration for my blog posts while I am swimming or driving, so I consider these to be sacred times.

Once in the water, I prefer to swim in the lane closest to the wall and farthest from the entrance. I find facing the wall, helps me keep my focus to listen to God, rather than the flailing arms and legs in the nearby lanes.

I noticed, however, that the pool became more and more crowded in the morning; in fact, it seems to be jam-packed with people. Day after day, I arrive to take whatever lane was available.

But I also began to notice that day after day, just as I would start to get in the only open lane, a certain man would run ahead of me and throw his stuff in! He obviously saw me; he essentially had to push me aside to take the spot. It made me want to punch him in the face! Once again restraining myself from violently kicking the man, I ended up stepping back to wait for another lane to become available.

How does this frustrating experience relate to God's sovereignty in the microcosm? Well, after each time this gentleman bounded into the pool in front of me, the far lane – the one I preferred! – would open up. It was as if the Lord was thrusting His hand in my way, saying, "Wait John, I have something better for you."

Now I have to be honest: On each of these occasions I still had to work through forgiving this guy. A roundhouse kick to his head would have been cathartic! But without his rudeness, I would not have had this amazing revelation. Knowing that God used him to show me His sovereignty was a huge revelation.

SOVEREIGN MOVE OF SOVEREIGNTY

How many circumstances in life reveal to us the tenderness of God's Sovereign Touch? How often does God's plan include our inconvenience for our benefit? How many apparent diversions are actually God's loving hand positioning us to carry out His purpose? It takes great faith to see God in action, because in the moment it can seem like just some jerk is trying to cheat us.

It is vital for us to remember, "Blessed is he who is not offended in Me" (Matthew 11:6). God's sovereignty will almost never involve my uncontested ease.

Seeing God's Sovereign Touch enacted in our everyday lives is all about faith. It requires complete trust in the Father and His ability to lead us through every circumstance. Our situation may appear hopeless, offensive, or simply a waste of time, but trusting in God will lead us to the experience of His Life and His divine Purpose in our lives.

If we choose to stay in the Tree of Knowledge, judging everything as good or evil, we will miss God's personal care in the seemingly "little" scenarios of our lives. If we do not want to miss God or His plans, we must learn to embrace His ways, more and more, even when they challenge or inconvenience us. What a grand adventure!

And we know that for those who love God all things work together for good, for those who are called according to his purpose.
Romans 8:28 ESV

Many are the plans in the mind of a man, but it is the purpose of the Lord that will stand.
Proverbs 19:21 ESV

The Lord has established His throne in the heavens, and His kingdom rules over all.
Psalm 103:19 ESV

Great Big Woolly Booger

God showed up in the microcosm on another occasion. Martha and I were having dinner at a restaurant that seated its guests family-style. We were shown to a table for four, with the potential for one or two strangers to join us. It all depended on the luck of the draw, for the secular person, or a sovereign choosing, for the person of faith. Which person would I be?

We'd just settled into our places when a large, hairy, biker walked into the restaurant. I noticed a long, fuchsia-red ponytail hanging off his shoulder. He wore camo pants and a black leather vest, and he looked like a great big woolly booger.

Blinded by his appearance I muttered, "Oh no!" anticipating a less than pleasant meal. And sure enough, guess who was seated at our table? Yep, the woolly booger!

But when we greeted our new table-mate, his face lit up like a Christmas tree. He opened up to us, sharing his huge, beautiful heart. He was an anomaly: Yes, he rode a Harley Davidson and enjoyed a shot or two of Jack Daniels with dinner. But guess what else? He was also the principal tuba player for a symphony orchestra!

Martha asked him to name his favorite composer. I would have guessed The Grateful Dead or Korn, but to my surprise he responded, "Prokofiev." As he described his passion for music, he blossomed with beauty, like a fragrant desert flower. He discussed the Star Wars score with such appreciation that I thought he might tear up. He noted how the music moved the audience to see battle cruisers flying overhead or to feel the moment when Princess Leia falls in love with Han

The Sovereign Touch

Solo.

In God's sovereignty, our Father wanted to delight Martha and me with this deeply emotive and artistic man. He made our dinner memorable! In fact, he was exactly the kind of person I would have been drawn to and chosen to sit with for dinner. What surprising from an unexpected quarter! This is a sovereign lesson: never shut the door based on appearance. Our God, who does not judge based on externals, just might be concealing internal sophistication!

No, I am not necessarily going to snuggle up with the next bearded vagrant I see, looking for a gem. But I am going to trust my God to move circumstances, big AND small, so that I can be delighted in Him. I am going to trust His sovereign touches in my life. Who knows? He might reveal even more hidden treasures like that precious woolly booger!

Portrait of a Life

As one last example of God's sovereignty at work, I want to tell you the story behind my self-portrait, which I used on the front cover of *Where Are You, God?* – my recently published testimony. I think it's a dynamic and special painting, but is that just because it is a picture of me? No, my self-portrait is dynamic because it is a revelation that God can move us into places quite unbeknownst to us. He leads us, as a Shepherd, while we slowly pass through the pastures of our lives.

Not only did God prove Himself as Lord of my actions, but He also used those actions to maneuver me to know Him, see Him, and come to Him. This is the most hopeful thing! We are not simply on a Mister Toad's Wild Ride of human chaos and vague wanderings. Jesus Christ is truly Lord and sovereign.

A Prophetic Picture

My father took a picture of me when I was 11 months old. He artistically posed me and used dramatic lighting, which helped add depth and meaning to the photograph. But more importantly, the Lord used my then-unsaved dad to set up a visual representation for a prophetic vision of my life. It's utterly fascinating to me. And as I share the back-story with you, maybe then you can see the personal implication for your own life and happenings as well.

Years ago, it became really important to me, for some reason, to have a painting of this picture. My artistic medium has always been photography, so I did not have the ability to paint it. But I found another artist who was willing to do an art swap. She received one of my framed fine art photographs and agreed to paint my baby portrait in oils.

I waited months and then years for my painting, to no avail. Even though she took delivery of my piece, she clearly was not going to come through for me. Then, to stack insult upon injury, this artist lost the only copy I had of my baby portrait. All I had left was an iPhone snapshot of it and a huge desire to see it painted.

So what does a man do with these parameters? Well, I decided to paint it myself! I now praise God that this woman reneged on our deal. No one else would have had the passion to communicate His sovereign message but me. If she had kept up her end of the bargain, I perhaps would have received a nice oil painting and that would have been it. I would have hung it on my wall and enjoyed it, but I would've lost the divine journey and message, which God had intended from the beginning.

BECOMING A PAINTER

I went to painting classes for over nine years before gaining
the level of skill needed to paint my picture. Even when I
lost sight of the goal and forgot what I was doing it all for, it
turned out that all my paintings and drawings were for this
end — to become good enough so that I could one day paint
this image. I refused to have it look amateurish. It not only
had to carry the quality of art but also the message I believe
God wanted to communicate through it.

My first art teacher taught me about finding the message behind your painting and communicating that. Literally every
drawing and painting had to have the elements of meaning.
This was perfect for what I wanted to accomplish. Then my
next teacher taught me how to accomplish this through a
painterly feel while giving me the confidence to move forward in my own style. These lessons weren't just exercises
for me; they were a mission with a purpose.

AN 'UGLY' BABY WITH DIVINE PURPOSE

After years of training and preparation, I was ready to tackle my painting goal. I sketched out the image and prepared
to begin painting when a fellow student came over and
mocked it. She said, "At least you're drawing an ugly baby
well."

Satan tipped his hand with this comment. If ever before I
thought it was just a painting for me to enjoy, now I knew I
was motivated the whole time by God. I praise God for this
cruel woman; her attack gave me that much more passion to
paint my picture and do it well. I knew that this was not a
mere painting; it truly had a divine purpose.

Over the last 50 years of my life, God orchestrated a path for a message and He does the same for us all. Everything happened while I was still in the dark about God's plan: the Lord used my dad to take the picture, then gave me a heart to value it, and finally used others to devalue it so that I would love it that much more.

Jesus gave me passion to learn to paint and the boldness to attempt to paint this image. He gifted me with the ability and teaching to do it His way. He gave me the testimony to publish, and then called me to use my painting as its cover. How fitting that the testimony about my life would be represented by an image that exemplified the message in those pages. I was directed as God orchestrated: my motives, my actions, and my results.

The pain of being cheated hurt, and the horror of having my original photograph lost made me angry. The work to learn to paint was costly, and the mockery of others was painful. But God's purpose superseded all of that. His plan was in place and it was being played out without my knowing. Alone with a thread or two of pain, God weaves in our lives things to make Himself known. I never knew the picture would reveal my path of seeking God. I can't even say that my motivation to have this photograph painted emanated from me. Not knowing where any of it would lead, I just walked out my life as the Lord led. But behind the scenes, as always is true, God was maneuvering and bringing about His plan.

You may not currently see God's movement in your life. You may be questioning, as I was, "Where are You, God?" Our moments and movements sometimes feel random and arbitrary. But it's my earnest belief that God is weaving a tapestry of our lives to give us every opportunity to know Him.

Don't Look at What is Happening

Several years ago my sister suffered through a bout with cancer. I prayed earnestly and often for her healing.

In response to my prayers, God told me, "Don't look at what is happening. Look at what I am doing!"

I cannot tell you how liberating this revelation was! We humans tend to focus on the particular circumstances we are facing. In actuality, however, something higher and bigger is taking place: the working out of God's purposes.

I remember another instance of testing in this arena of faith. Martha Kilpatrick and I were traveling to a conference on standby tickets. While it can be an inconvenience, it does save money, especially when you are traveling last minute. The deal with standby tickets is this: If there is an extra seat available on the flight you want to take, you fly. If not, you wait. Naturally, this can be a bit nerve-wracking, because you usually do not know until the very last moment.

On this trip, God was kind enough not to leave me hanging. "You're not going to make this flight," He told me.

I did not say out loud, "Why God?" But I was certainly thinking it, and God knew it.

"To test your anxiety levels," He answered me. "Will you trust Me?"

I sat waiting as the ticket agents called name after name, hoping for better but already knowing what would happen. We did not get on.

Then the next flight rolled around. God spoke again. "You'll get on this one," He said. "Was that Him," I wondered, "or my own desire?"

We made the flight. God had told me! And as I sat in seat 24B with Martha to my left, God reminded me, "Don't look at what is happening. Look at what I'm doing!"

Circumstances can seem momentous when they push against God's purposes. We are vulnerable to our Creator. Nothing happens outside His control. Look at this passage from Isaiah 45:

So all the world from east to west will know there is no other God. I am the LORD, and there is no other. I create the light and make the darkness. I send good times and bad times. I, the LORD, am the one who does these things.
Isaiah 45:6-7 NLT

That whole chapter of Isaiah is indicting. God is over ALL! That includes everything from planes to cancer, families to personal struggles. Nothing happens beyond His control. This is both comforting and terrifying. My God is in control – period, end of story.

When I am tempted to fret or fear, I am called to entreat my Abba, my Creator, as the One who is in control. He promised not to leave me or forsake me. I am shepherded by my Good Shepherd regardless of what is happening, regardless of the circumstances around me.

Even to your old age I am He, and even to hair white with age will I carry you. I have made, and I will bear; yes, I will carry and will save you.
Isaiah 46:4 AMP

Corrupt Authority and Government

Every now and again when you look at life from a certain angle, it seems as if evil and wrong and legalized iniquity are having it all their own way and you feel that everything must go to pieces; but it doesn't; around it is the sovereignty of God.

Oswald Chambers
Scottish Baptist and Holiness Movement evangelist, teacher, author
1874 - 1917

For through Him God created everything
 in the heavenly realms and on earth.
He made the things we can see
 and the things we can't see —
such as thrones, kingdoms, rulers, and authorities in the unseen world.
 Everything was created through Him and for Him.
Colossians 1:16 NLT

Rise and Bow

It is extremely trying to our souls to have to accept and receive an authority God has placed over us, especially when we immensely disagree with them. Authorities, leaders, and governmental officials can try our very core, particularly when they run roughshod over our rights.

How does God's sovereignty relate when we encounter this in our work, church, or elsewhere? Nothing so perfectly reveals our rebellious heart as being powerless to influence those in power over us. It is exceptionally chafing when these powers, which are intended to represent and protect our values, our rights, and our very selves, do quite the opposite.

And while this is true, God's use of authority is intended to challenge us. Authority exposes the heart of every man. Authority is the greatest confrontation of God's sovereignty. It is unavoidable – governments and delegated authority test our willingness to trust God's sovereign hand and Lordship.

I occasionally enjoy systematically going through three books of the Bible: Judges and I and II Kings. I simply start at the beginning and follow the path of the Jewish people. Without fail, God always speaks to me with something that relates to my current life, a fresh insight from ancient Words that relates to my today.

Looking at the Book of Judges. We see repeatedly witness the evil the Israelites committed in the sight of the Lord. As a result, He handed them over to an enemy for discipline, hoping to effect a change.

The last time I scoured these passages for His thoughts and

mind, I believe I heard Him say, "Don't rise, *bow* to Me!" I knew He was speaking about our government in the United States; how, while many agree and many disagree with our leadership, this struggle was put into place by our Sovereign God.

Further, if we understand that every person in a position of authority was placed there by God, then God must be at the root of our struggles. It is hard to say otherwise, if we believe the Apostle Paul's letter to the Romans:

> *Everyone must submit to governing authorities. For all authority comes from God, and those in positions of authority have been placed there by God.*
> *Romans 13:1 NLT*

The next logical question is how do I respond?

What I have learned from my Israeli brothers (several centuries removed) is to bow and cry out to God. Our job is to bow down to the Lord of our rights and seek His face (see 2 Chronicles 7:14). Our position of surrender and yieldedness to God as God is more dynamic than even our vote or protests. God does not need to see my raised fist. No, He needs my neck bowed in surrender and prayer to Him.

I do not know if we can stay the inevitable judgment of God on our nation, but I do know that God is our Answer.

As Martha Kilpatrick puts it, "When God shakes all things, the obedient stand intact and the disobedient collapse in ruin."[1]

---

1 Kilpatrick, Martha, Kingdom Safety, Copyright © 2003, 2013 - Shulamite Publishing INC.

What Lurks Behind Our Resistance?

Every generation witnesses some degree of civil unrest. Some that stand out in my life time are the Stonewall riots, Ashbury Park race riots, L.A. Rodney King riots, Occupy Wall Street, Ferguson, and the list goes on and on. Since our nations foundation we have experienced civil unrest. It seems to be the ebb and flow of humanity. But in light of the unrest I have witnessed, I would like to share with you how I personally sought the Lord for answers.

My heart was heavy and saddened by the riots and corruption in our land. One night, I had a disturbing dream. The dream was about aggressive, intimidating men, filled with strife and violence. At one point during my dream, I walked into a dark room packed with men – thugs who were ready to erupt. It woke me up and I could not go back to sleep.

The next morning, I turned to God to still my heart and settle my fears. He led me to Romans 13, which speaks of respecting authority because all authority comes from God. So thinking back to the Book of Judges, while God puts leadership in place for judgment, it is also deeply necessary and often out of our direct control.

CASTING OFF THE RESTRAINTS OF AUTHORITY

When we cast off the restraints of our God, rejecting His rule over us, we are subject to consequences. And so I ask, just whose authority are we truly trying to shake off in our resistance?

Zooming out and away from single events or even one particular country; I am speaking of the primal rebellion that sets up human rebellion in the first place. The truth behind the anarchy of the world: In our hearts we have cast off the restraints of God, so now we are unable to submit to the human authorities He places over us. Lawlessness runs rampant because in the secret of each of our hearts, we resist God. Our issue is not from resistance to man; but resistance to God.

But some of His people hated Him and sent Him their declaration of independence, stating that they had rebelled and would not acknowledge Him as their King.
Luke 19:14 TLB

I will have no ability to submit to human authority when I resent and resist God's actual authority in my life. In this heart condition, rebellion, godlessness, anarchy, and unrest can thrive. We see this throughout the course of history, men and women had to bow to unjust leaders. Within both the Old and New Testaments, Israel had to face the cruelty of unjust rulers. From Pharaoh to Rome and all those in between, our resistance is punished. This is what it looks like when we are working to be free from God's rule. This is the direct result of telling God to shut up.

"We don't want this man to rule over us!"
Luke 19:14b HCSB

If there is no authority that is in place but by God's own direction, then God is to blame. Our fight is with God! This makes us hugely vulnerable to Him. And I think this is precisely the struggle. I do not want to be so weak that I can be hurt by His choice, but I am.

We want authority and sovereignty to be about man, not God. I can fight, spit at, and revile a man, but God? My rocks cannot reach Him. The entire climate of our world is the result of man being mad as hell that God is actually God. We are infuriated that He has the audacity to reign in our lives. We are witnessing daily the fruit of a culture that has been so blessed by God that now we feel we do not need Him, nor do we want His meddling influence in our lives and choices. And while He does not expect us to always be happy with His choice for our authority, we still have to recognize it is His doing.

Instead, clothe yourself with the presence of the Lord Jesus Christ. And don't let yourself think about ways to indulge your evil desires.
Romans 13:14 NLT

Authority is a vital subject we each must face with honesty and clarity. God's sovereignty and authority work hand and hand, we cannot accept one without the other. To reject authority is to reject God, and to receive His authority is to receive Him as Lord.

Cursing Delegated Authority

Consequently, the one who resists authority is opposing what God has set in place, and those who do so will bring judgment on themselves.
Romans 13:2 NKJV

Reviling authority is no joking matter. If you look in the Old Testament, cursing authority results in leprosy, plagues, the earth swallowing the one who curses, and other means of death, to name a few. In the New Testament, blindness, degradation and dropping dead result from cursing authority. While cursing authority might feel cathartic in the moment, like yelling at someone who cut you off in the car, the result is the same. It is neither helpful nor changes the leader.

We humans cannot curse authority and avoid reaping disastrous consequences. It is further than mere murmuring. But literally to speak curses against those to whom God has delegated authority is to unleash a whirlwind of destruction back upon our own lives.

I know many who have so resisted God's choice of an authority in their lives, that they not only became a bitter version of themselves but they actually became worse than their leaders. Their resistance was a pushing away from God and into becoming what they cursed in others. Life destruction was the result.

Through this, the devil achieves his goal of devouring, stealing, killing and destroying God's beloved humans (see I Peter 5:8; John 10:10). Satan loves to involve God's own creation in bringing about an implosion, and reviling authority is a debacle of destruction.

When humans curse authority, it is a win-win for Satan. Why? Because either the devil wins by hindering God's delegated authority, or he wins when revilers of authority reap destruction in their own lives.

You shall not revile God, nor curse the ruler of your people.
Exodus 22:28

In his book Spiritual Authority, Watchman Nee writes "Whenever there is rebellion and reviling among us we shall lose the presence of God….." He also says, "No one can reject God's delegated authority with one hand and receive God with the other hand." This is frightening because it means the progress of a man's spiritual life is halted when reviling is present! Again, Satan wins.

Remind the believers to be subject to rulers and authorities, to be
obedient and ready for every good work, to malign no one, and to
be peaceable and gentle, showing full consideration to everyone.
Titus 3:1-2 BSB

The Power of Living Under Authority

What is the power of living under a leader you neither like nor agree with? Many of us curse and rail about the leadership that God Himself has placed us under. My disagreement with my leaders does not justify my reviling their authority. Disagreeing with my leaders does not justify my reviling their authority.

In Christ, I am rich regardless of what my authority does or does not do. It is my responsibility to pray for the leaders God placed over me. With this comes the promise that we can live peaceful and quiet lives marked by godliness and dignity (1 Timothy 2:2).

Once a leader is in their place over me, I have been properly introduced to God's own choice. "Let everyone be subject to the governing authorities, for there is no authority except that which God has established. The authorities that exist have been established by God" (Romans 13:1 NIV).

When I submit and surrender to God's choice, a brilliant world opens up to me. I can come into a "Daniel" from the Bible reality. A reality where every knee will bow before the Lord, regardless of political party or human agenda, regardless of how it looks in the moment.

True men of God like Daniel and David lived in difficult situations, not beneath their circumstances but rather over it all in Him. I can often mentally clean up the stories of these Bible character's lives. I can forget that these humans had real prolonged struggles and yet by faith were victorious.

Daniel lived under Nebuchadnezzar, a cruel and tyrannical king. This crisis made Daniel rather than defeating him.

Daniel was given the riches of the Kingdom, IN his fire.

In God's purpose and plan, Nebuchadnezzar served to bless Daniel and train him to rule and reign from the heavens. If Daniel had cursed or rebelled against his wicked leader, he would have never received the treasure God was desiring to bestow on him. He was being given an eternal reward and heavenly position within his trouble.

While we may or may not agree with our authorities and leaders, could it be that God is wishing to give us a gift IN the adversity? Could the political stage that causes us such angst be the very vehicle of delivery to give us an eternal reward and blessing? Are we being called to a vision beyond mere despots and potentates? Are we being trained for an eternal position in a temporal situation? And if our climate was not so polarized, chaotic and unpredictable, would we be given the training we need to rule and reign with Christ forever?

I can get just as crazy as anyone watching the three ring circus of politics. I can fume and rail when things go in a direction I believe is incorrect. I can sit dumbfounded with my mouth hanging wide open when I hear the rhetoric and spin that seems more destructive than constructive. And all the while God has set up a training ground of my testing and proving.

Daniel was *made* in Babylon. David was *forged* in the wilderness. And each of us too will be *formed* in our own fire of forming.

To curse the adversity is to curse the very place and stage that is set in place to make me who I will be with Christ throughout eternity.

What About Corrupt Authorities?

What should the people do when authority is corrupt? In this fallen world, where none are good, we find men coming into power and it is their fallenness that rises to meet the challenge.

> "Power tends to corrupt, and absolute power corrupts absolutely. Great men are almost always bad men...."
> Lord John Dalberg-Acton
> English Catholic historian, politician, and writer
> 1834 - 1902

How are we to deal with this reality? Because this is the human condition, let's look how those in the Bible handled this very thing.

Daniel, David, Esther, Joseph, each handled corrupt authorities in much the same way; none of them retaliated by reviling, complaining, or scorning these authorities. Through their testimonies, we are given direction. So how did they do it?

These individuals lived in a higher realm. They lived above the machinations of man, untouched in their core by the extremes of wickedness. Each of them experienced the pain of living under corrupt authorities, while standing firm in the Light of The Authority. They all had a Kingdom view and lived above the fray.

We too can live like this. Our intended position is living from the heavens.

Corrupt authorities affect our lives. Our only solution is to seek the Authority above all other authorities. He is God over all, not just those who call themselves His.

Do I just let authority hurt me? Did, Daniel, David, Joseph or Esther? Daniel was thrown into a lion's den to be eaten and his faithful friends were thrown into a burning furnace. David was hunted like a dog with the intent of murder. Joseph was wrongfully accused of attempted rape and left in prison to rot. Esther stood as God's choice living as one of many wives of a cruel king, while political forces attempted to wipe the earth of the Jewish people.

Were these men and women ultimately hurt? Because Daniel lived under God's Authority, while his corrupt earthly authority set the world ablaze, he saw the heavens rule on earth. While David's earthly king sought to kill him, the Higher Authority established his throne forever. Although Joseph's godless pharaoh ruled the land, he would save his people from great famine. And Esther while being married to a tyrannical husband and king, saved the Jewish people from a genocide. Corrupt authorities have no sway on the hearts of those loyal to God's Authority, and God does His Will for those who surrender.

If our value system and worth is found solely in this earthly plain, we will be leveled. Corrupt authorities will abuse, discourage and destroy us. But if we live under the authority of the King of Kings, He will work things together for something so much higher than just this temporal plain. While His Kingdom rule will be seen over this earth, what's more an eternal value will be set upon our lives, and ultimately those corrupt authorities will be transformed or ultimately taken out. It requires faith in The Ruler, Jesus Christ who is Lord.

It is impossible to live in this world without facing corrupt authorities. The good news is that as our face is turned to God's ultimate authority our yielding to Him will not be in vain. No, just because I submit to the King's authority, it does not mean I will not have confrontations with the corrupt or evil authorities of our land. But the view beyond the moment will reveal His Lordship even in the corruption. He has the last word always even with the corrupt in power.

For it is commendable if someone bears up under the pain of unjust suffering because they are conscious of God.
1 Peter 2:19 NIV

Can You Hear Me *Now*?

We think that governmental order is just a secular expression but actually it is very spiritual. Look in the Bible. Those who were set in the place of authority were put there by God to communicate His thoughts. When the nation of Israel played the harlot with the world, an oppressive regime took them over. And when they repented and sought the face of God, He placed leaders over them to lead them in righteousness. We might not immediately see or understand God's plan, but it's important for us to know that He is sovereign. Back and forth, the ebb and flow of governmental bodies are chosen by God to communicate.

A governmental leadership actually reflects the heart of the people as much as the heart of the leader. When the people turned their faces towards God, He set in place rulers to deliver. When they turned away from His Life and commandments, a crushing regime was set in place.

Let every person be subject to the governing authorities. For there is no authority except from God [granted by His permission and sanction], and those which exist have been put in place by God.
Romans 13:1 AMP

I would love to think that my leaders are an island unto themselves, that they are not reflective of me at all. I would love to think that if the character of my leaders is bad, it has nothing to do with me. But this just is not so! Our lives and choices determine our leaders.

When we individually or nationally refuse to listen to God, He turns up the heat to get our attention. God is a Vice Grip of Love crunching the bone. It is amazing how clear our hearing can get when we are in pain.

With our politicians not listening to their constituents, nations refusing to hear and abide by God's law, and individuals living willfully, plugging their ears to His Voice. Could God just be setting leaders in place to get our attention? Is His response to our deafness a bold statement of, "Can you hear Me now?"

When Authority Makes Demands Against God

How do Christians handle it in countries where the state sanctioned "religion" forbid things like: owning a Bible, meeting in homes, or preaching unsanctioned doctrine? Am I to follow the atheism sanctioned by authority just because they are my God given authority?

Look at the Peoples Republic of China who looks to protect its citizens from things that do not conform to "normal religious activities," generally understood to refer to only religions that submit to state control. If the narrative is not theirs, you cannot speak it. Their Constitution further forbids the use of religion to "engage in activities that disrupt social order, impair the health of citizens or interfere with the educational system of the state." All sound good at face value but the Gospel of the Kingdom violates every one of these rules.

The Gospel preached by Christ was highly disruptive to social order, removed impediments to the health of the people, and interfered with the sanctioned rules and orders laid out by man. The Gospel ran counter to the religious and governmental structures of the day and still does.

How do we handle the paradox? What do we do when the government God put in place forbids that we do what the Bible commands? For instance, these Chinese Christians are not allowed to follow any religion that preaches doctrine counter to the state. Yet the Gospel preaches the Kingdom of GOD, which is seen as a competing ruling force. It is in our day, just like it was in Christ's. They believed Jesus was a subversive leader, setting up government to overthrow the Romans.

Some believe they can out lawyer the Bible in this, deciding the judicial bounds of authority. "Here is where government rules and NO further! That is your space to govern and this is mine!" A separation between Church and state. But this is a slippery slope, because what was intended to protect the churches rights, is now used to confine it from influence. The Church is supposed to be influential! We are actually commanded to make disciples of the nations. Nations not just individuals.

When I set myself up as judge, ruling between two apparent contradictory sides of scripture, I am attempting to be The Judge. I was never intended to be the scale on which the Word rests, the Lord Almighty is the fulcrum, which is based on His Mind, not mine. My job is to inquire and listen to His mind.

Christ is Lord of All! And all means ALL! (see Ephesians 1:22, Philippians 2:9-11) And while this is an immutable fact, we are also commanded by Him to be subject to governing authorities (see Romans 13 and 1 Peter 2). In 1 Peter 2:18 he says, "not only to those who are good and gentle, but also to those who are unreasonable." How in the world do we justify this great quandary?

All authority has been given to Me in heaven and on earth.
Matthew 28:18 HCSB

THREADING THE NEEDLE OF AUTHORITY

You would have no authority over Me,
unless it had been given you from above.
John 19:11 ESV

Here is the bottom line of authority. It is impossible to navigate without God. We cannot maneuver authority on our own. Only Christ can thread the authority needle – skillfully navigating through a difficult conflict. I am not intended to base my submission to authority on how I feel, what my opinion is, or what I think are my rights. That is independence from God and eating from the Tree of the Knowledge of Good and Evil. This will ALWAYS be death to my life.

But there is good news, actually GREAT NEWS. His Life and Will lives within me. And as I let Jesus live through me, He not only threads the authority needle, but works a living tapestry of His Life and Will through me.

> *"We must obey God rather than men."*
> *Acts 5:29 ESV*

Jesus is Supreme Ruler and He looks for me to seek His Will in all my actions. No, He never violates His Word because He is the Word. But as the Word, my surrender to Him is paramount. That being said, He never asked me to independently trek out on my own to figure it out. He never said, "I gave you a brain and a Book, now go figure it out." Quite the contrary, He gave me Himself and His Life. He calls me to live in dependence, not independently of Him.

Thinking that I know, will lead me to exalt my thoughts and opinions above the Most High every time. (See 2 Corinthians 10:5) Again, Jesus cannot violate the Bible, because He is the Word. So I cannot choose what I want and do not want in His Word or that I think I can live by the Voice and neglect the Word. God lives His Life through me and His Life as my life is able to live under authority.

I have been crucified with Christ and I no longer live, but Christ lives in me. The life I now live in the body, I live by faith in the Son

> *of God, who loved me and gave Himself for me.*
> Galatians 2:20 NIV

CONSEQUENCES OF THE LIFE OF CHRIST

Persecution of the church has historically come from secular governments and false religion. Most of Christian martyrs have died because they refused to obey such authorities. And I can guarantee that those who live by the Indwelt Life of Christ will receive persecution. "If they persecuted Me, they will also persecute you" John 15:20. Persecution is part of the blessing found in the beatitudes. But with the hatred and persecution is a great promise, "YOUR REWARD IN HEAVEN WILL BE GREAT!" (See Matthew 5:11-12)

Am I willing to pay the price to let Christ and His Life emanate through my life? Regardless of the consequences, is my commitment to His Will above my own will?

When the initial shut down over the Covid-19 Pandemic happened, I had questions. With something occurring so momentous, could this just be God's hand at work? Everything from sports to schools, churches to funerals shut down, I asked God, "What are YOU doing?" I knew the magnitude of a complete national shutdown was too colossal to not have a Sovereign Source. And I say this all the while believing that the machinations of man could very well be a contributing factor.

My question was, "What are YOU doing?" I do not say this to elevate myself, if anything it reveals my deep dependence on the mind and Will of Christ. Quite frankly, I wanted to be in line with Him and His Will during this time. I had to ask because I would not know if I did not ask.

Many thoughts and questions ran through my spirit. What if our Sovereign God is using this virus to shut us down because of our great idolatry? Could God be preventing us from focusing on things that have captured our attention from Him? Is He preventing our churches from meeting because our focus has veered away from Jesus as Source and onto the entertaining institution itself? Have our sporting events and concerts obscured our devotion and focus from *Him*?

Our inquiry is a necessity, because we have a relational God. If I went full steam ahead defending my rights, could I not just be struggling with God Himself? You see, we must always seek God's mind and Will or we are mandating our laws on life that will result in death. If I have made a law into "we should meet hell or high water," I might miss the actual message the Lord was proclaiming.

My fellow believers, when it seems as though you are facing nothing but difficulties, see it as an invaluable opportunity to experience the greatest joy that you can!
James 1:2 TPT

I am not telling you what to believe or how to view the events around the pandemic. What I am contending for is that our first response in life is to inquire of our Sovereign God. He is so ready to reveal His Life and Will and so yearns that His children would know Him.

God's Sovereignty in Wrath

Not only have we witnessed the fury of God on the authorities abusing their God-given position, but we have also seen the retribution awaiting those who rebel against and revile God's authorities.

Let's look at an aspect of God's sovereignty that is squirm-worthy, and it has to do with the wrath of God seen in the life of Jonah from the Bible.

Jonah was an Israelite who lived approximately 800 B.C. to 750 B.C., during one of the many times when the nation of Israel claimed to stand for God, while being completely against Him in their actual hearts and lives. As a result of their sins, by God's sovereign hand the nation was later (722 B.C.) treated severely and cruelly occupied by a neighboring nation: Assyria. Jonah's experience of God's sovereignty expresses the whole gamut: the reality, the repercussions, the resistance, the revelation and the receiving of sovereignty. It is a perfect picture of our struggle with the fact that God is God and God is sovereign.

Jonah, you may remember, was called by God in about 790-785 B.C. to "go to the great city of Nineveh [located in the nation of Assyria] and preach against it, because its wickedness has come up before Me" (Jonah 1:1). Jonah resisted taking the life and Word of God to the Ninevites. In fact, his actions and words demonstrated that he would rather die than to obey God's direction. Why? Was he just that willful, rebellious and headstrong?

No, but there was a reason Jonah (whose name, interestingly enough, meant "dove") behaved in a way that was anything but dove-like. We are given a clue to this reason from the archaeological background of the Assyrians of his time:

"The merciless cruelty of his campaigns is the constant boast of Ashur-nasir-pal II: 'I stormed the mountain peaks and took them. In the midst of the mighty mountain I slaughtered them, with their blood I dyed the mountain red like wool. With the rest of them I darkened the gullies and precipices of the mountains. I carried off their spoil and their possessions. The heads of the warriors I cut off, and I formed them into a pillar over against their city, their young men and their maidens I burned in the fire.

"'I built a pillar over against the city gate, and I flayed all the chief men who had revolted, and I covered the pillar with their skins; some I walled up within the pillar, some I impaled upon the pillar on stakes, and others I bound to stakes round about the pillar; many within the border of my own land I flayed, and I spread their skins upon the walls; and I cut off the limbs of the officers, of the royal officers who had rebelled.'"[2]

Jonah gave his hatred of the Ninevites merit because of Assyrian's acts of satanic evil against his people. Which one of us would not? Think back to 2001 – how many of us would have called our attitude toward the 9-11 terrorists "righteous anger"?

Nineveh was not just a city full of people with different ideologies or contested borders. These folks – or at least their rulers and military leaders – were barbarians with a demonic taste for blood. The Assyrians had slaughtered Beth Arbel,

---

2 Light From the Ancient Past: The Archaeological Background of Judaism and Christianity, Jack Finegan, Princeton University Press, second printing, 1974, p. 202-203.

a city in Israel, in much the fashion described above.[3] The Ninevites were monsters!

Now we understand why a man named "Dove" could be so stridently opposed to God's will for Nineveh. Jonah was deeply wounded by the Assyria's for their harassment and cruelty of his people in the past. How could a man with a gentle nature not be wounded? And horrified and terrified! But God does not put limits on His willingness to show mercy and forgive, not for the evil Assyrians and not for any of us!

---

3 Elwell, W. A., & Beitzel, B. J. (1988). Shalmaneser. In Baker Encyclopedia of the Bible (Vol. 2, p. 1935). Grand Rapids, MI: Baker Book House. See also: Astour, Michael C. "841 B. C.: The First Assyrian Invasion of Israel." Journal of the American Oriental Society, vol. 91, no. 3, 1971, pp. 383–389.

Judgment and the Heavenly Man

Martha said to me one day, "The whole process of becoming a heavenly man is in letting go of what God has already taken and giving what He is asking for."

As I studied the life of Jonah I realized that this process fit Jonah's issue to a tee. Jonah was thinking his own thoughts, rather than following God and God's thoughts in his situation. And because his thoughts were his own, and not God's, he acted as a natural man rather than a heavenly one.

It is so easy to think our own thoughts. We usually have a strong commitment to what we think. Jonah's story displays how devastating this can be. The good news is that God is committed to get His man into His mind and out of his own thoughts.

We looked at the history behind Jonah's hatred of the Assyrians, but what I did not look at was God in the macrocosm. It is not hard to understand why Jonah would resist being a messenger to a people who brutally and grotesquely massacred the Israelite city of Beth Arbel, but here is a wrench to throw into the gears: God's Sovereign Hand. Why were the Assyrians given permission to brutalize the house of Israel mercilessly?

After much rebellion against God, worshiping Baal under Ahab and Jezebel and not giving ear to His Prophets, the entire city of Beth Arbel was brutally wiped out in 841 BC.[4] The attack was so horrifying, that almost a century later, Hosea used it to illustrate the frightening judgment that

4 Myers, A. C. (1987). In The Eerdmans Bible dictionary (p. 931). Grand Rapids, MI: Eerdmans.

awaited Israel if they did not repent. "Therefore tumult shall arise among your people, And all your fortresses shall be plundered As Shalman plundered Beth Arbel in the day of battle—A mother dashed in pieces upon her children" (Hos. 10:14).

The horror of Beth Arbel did not come out of nowhere. Israel abandoned all the commandments of the LORD their God. They sold themselves to do evil in the sight of the LORD, provoking Him to anger: Under Ahab and then his son, Joram, Israel had turned her back on God. And God used her enemy to scourge her.

The House of Israel certainly experienced God's wrath at the hands of the Assyrians, but wrath is the last expression of God's love. The beginning of judgment happens long before we experience His punitive actions. This mercy is actually evident in Beth Arbel's fall. That was the fall of only one city in Israel, not the entire nation. God's grace extended another 120 years before the whole nation fell under the sword of Assyria.

Judgment is the breaking of God's heart to relinquish us to our own desires. This is God sorrowfully allowing us to exercise our free will to leave Him. Sovereignty and free will work in conjunction with and not opposition to one another.

Jonah followed his thoughts in two ways: one, in his bitterness with Nineveh (the capital city of Assyria) for their cruelty, and two, in anger with how God chose to judge the House of Israel. This is a side of God most wish to deny. But a sovereign God does circumstantially use situations and people to judge and chastise His children.

JUDGMENT STARTS IN THE HOUSE OF THE LORD

Before we throw any stones at Israel's waywardness, we must remember that we Americans currently live in a nation that has quickly turned our backs on God to follow other gods. If the Kingdom of Israel was not spared, how can we believe that we will scoot under the wire?

Though we might not wish to believe in the wrath and judgment of God or in His sovereign use of destruction, it is real nonetheless. Why? *Because God is either sovereign over all or He isn't sovereign at all.*

In his bestselling book Christian Doctrine, Dr. Shirley Guthrie notes similarly: "If the God of the Christian faith is love, then God's wrath cannot be an alternative to love; it must be an expression of love."

God's wrath is simply another side of His deeply expressed love for us. It is not contrary to God's love, it IS His Love. This point is way too important to understanding sovereignty—especially in our culture today. [5]

---

5 Guthrie, Shirley, Christian Doctrine. Westminster/John Knox Press, Louisville, KY, C. 1994, pp.261.

Believing God is an Unjust Judge

Jonah struggled with his perception that God was unjust, believing He was asking too much of him to deliver a message of forgiveness and love to his enemies. He saw God's willingness to offer mercy to the Ninevites as suspect: How could God be so unjust to His own people as to offer kindness to their enemies?

Since the beginning of time, all of mankind has harbored suspicions of God. Quite frankly, we have approached God as if He wronged us, viewing Him as unjust. We believe that He is not good, and in fact at fault for the choices we made in the Garden.

This deceptive belief arose as a consequence of refusing to be satisfied with God's way, and instead seeking knowledge apart from God. In choosing this "coveted and superior knowledge" we traded Truth for the lie, believing Him to be something we ourselves are; *not good.*

When I struggled with my own suspicions about Him, God led me to Luke 18:

> *"[Jesus] then told them a parable on the need for them to pray always and not become discouraged: "There was a judge in a certain town who didn't fear God or respect man. And a widow in that town kept coming to him, saying, 'Give me justice against my adversary.'*

> *"For a while he was unwilling, but later he said to himself, 'Even though I don't fear God or respect man, yet because this widow keeps pestering me, I will give her justice, so she doesn't wear me out by her persistent coming.'"*

*Then the Lord said, "Listen to what the unjust judge says. Will not
God grant justice to His elect who cry out to Him day and night?
Will He delay to help them? I tell you that He will swiftly grant
them justice. Nevertheless, when the Son of Man comes, will He
find that faith on earth?"*
Luke 18:1-8 HCSB

For years I questioned why Jesus used an unjust judge,
apparently to represent the Heavenly Father, in one of His
parables. I knew that our Eternal Judge is completely just
even when we do not understand Him or His ways, but still,
why an unjust judge?

I understood the parable's lesson on persistent prayer: It was
obvious yet still convicting. But why use an unjust judge as
an example of the Eternal Father, rather than a just King?
After questioning and waiting for an answer from God, this
is what I heard:

Then the Lord said, Listen to what the unjust judge says!
Luke 18:6 AMPC

In the past, I believed that God was unjust and unfair—not
good. God used Martha Kilpatrick's booklet, *The Great Lie*, to
convict and set me free from my wrong thinking, which led
me to resolve my suspicions about Him. Here are two passages that reverberated in my heart.

"Your life is an expression of your idea of God.
Notice I didn't say, "Your idea is an expression of God."
I said, "Your life is an expression - of your idea - of God."
You are living out,
and living by,
and expressing,
and manifesting,

and creating… your concept of God.

You are like who you think He is.
You are just exactly like who you think He is.
So it is crucial that who you think He is, be the right perception."[6]

And another: "We were born with blasphemy in our genes, and it will surface in our reactions in a split second."

Oh, this booklet revealed to me the lie that lives in us today. This insidious lie born in Eden. I will not say that this lie does not attempt to creep back into my thinking during times of hardship and suffering, but I fight it now, rather than to accept it as fact.

You see, the parable of the unjust judge speaks not only about persistent prayer; it also speaks about the way in which we humans approach the Father, accusing Him of unjust treatment. Notice that in this story, the widow goes to an unjust judge rather than to a just King. Like this widow, we too have gone to God accusing Him of being unjust — rather than a sovereign king.

Unfortunately our lives often speak louder to us than what we know in our heads to be the truth of God's Word.

In this parable, Jesus tells us how we are to proceed with this faulty belief system towards Him; "Even though you believe Me to be cruel and unjust, come to Me like this." That is, come persistently, come regularly, don't stop asking. Test God's answers and actions against your own suspicions about Him.

---

6 Kilpatrick, Martha. *The Great Lie*. Pg 7 - 8 & 12.

In the end, not only did the man whom the widow believed to be an unjust judge receive his accuser – he answers her, and meets her need, as well. And the same is always true for the One we accuse of being unjust.

Truly our God is merciful! Even though we make false accusations against Him, He sovereignly leads us back to Himself!

PETITION THE MOST HIGH, NOT MAN

It is in us all to believe that God withholds and abuses power – to believe that He is unjust and unfair. This suspicion stems from our experiences and uncertainty with our earthly authorities. Whether the authorities are parents, bosses, law officers, or government officials, we stand as judges over God – after all, He put these leaders in place.

For all authority comes from God, and those in positions of authority have been placed there by God.
Romans 13:1 NLT

While despots may scheme and finagle, it is God Himself who places leaders in place. This is a vital lesson and one I cling to especially during election seasons. No man can steal what only God Himself endows.

We often see our leaders from the standpoint of their selfish or corrupt motives, which makes them unjust in our eyes. But our earthly leaders' motives are not our concern: We must grapple with the God's Will and Ways that put those authorities in their positions.

In America, we vote according to our conscience because this is our responsibility as citizens, but God will install as leaders those who are His choice, according to His Will. We must remind ourselves, sometimes repetitively, that God is over all earthly authority, that pushing against those in authority, is pushing against God's Plan. We can fund campaigns, post scalding curses online, or justify ourselves with various statistics—but this does nothing to thwart God's Will, He is God and He is Sovereign.

It is all too common for us to grumble and complain about our leaders and authorities at every level. I wish I was unscathed by this tendency, but alas, no. It is inherent in our frame as humans. And through the parable of the unjust judge, the Righteous King is asking us to petition Him. Persistent prayer is not thwarted by the limitations of our earthly kings: It rises above them to the Most High who is over them all!

What does that persistent prayer look like? Words like unabashed, bold, shameless, relentless, insistent, and impudent come to mind. Not the brazen boldness of entitlement, which is repugnant, but the faith of insistent pursuit that comes from knowing Jesus is my only Answer. Persistent prayer is more akin to humble desperation than arrogant demanding. I will go deeper into prayer later in the book.

The unjust judge is every man, every woman, every leader, because we are ALL unjust. There is no good in any human being, no, not one. All are corrupt. But it is not man that I petition, and neither do you. We have a Most High Sovereign King who cares, loves us, and brings to earth that which is found in Heaven.

Then He gave them an illustration to show that they must always pray and never lose heart...

Then the Lord said, "Notice how this dishonest magistrate behaved. Do you suppose God, patient as He is, will not see justice done for His chosen, who appeal to Him day and night? I assure you He will not delay in seeing justice done. Yet, when the Son of Man comes, will He find men on earth who believe in Him?"
Luke 18:1, 6-8 Phillips

But What About Free-Will?

Concerning God's sovereignty and our leaders, a good friend asked me, "What is man's role in sovereignty?" In other words, he was asking, "What about free will?"

Who hasn't asked this question? Men and women have been asking it since the beginning of time!

My answer: God is God! He is sovereign and nothing happens apart from Him, but man has free will to let his world go to rack and ruin through malicious willfulness or complacent neglect.

Everyone must submit to the governing authorities, for there is no authority except from God, and those that exist are instituted by God.
Romans 13:1 HCSB

It is our responsibility to pray for godly leaders and vote our conscience. And when God's choice of leaders is elected, I am called to pray for them to have wisdom "so that it may go well with me." (See 1 Timothy 2:1-4, Ephesian 6:3) This is the great paradox, one we will have to embrace as a whole. God is sovereign and our choice has power.

"It is a great privilege, as well as our responsibility, to pray for our government leaders."
Billy Graham

Here then is my charge: First, supplications, prayers, intercessions and thanksgivings should be made on behalf of all men: for kings and rulers in positions of responsibility, so that our common life may be lived in peace and quiet, with a proper sense of God and of

our responsibility to Him for what we do with our lives.
1 Timothy 2:2 Phillips

IS IT SOVEREIGNTY OR FREE WILL?

"I think that when you become a Christian, that primarily is the freedom that you receive, not just a freedom from, but a freedom to step into all that God has for you."[7]

Western Christians – and maybe Christians everywhere – typically want to embrace a black and white theology: Either sovereignty is total, or free will reigns. But God is not limited to a single aspect of our reality. Why? Because He is God. My only true struggle, then, is with the issue of His Lordship. Is He God, or am I?

My child, respect the Lord and the king. Don't join those people
who refuse to obey them.
Proverb 24:21 NCV

It will never make sense when I demand an answer. Here is some truth from Martha: "You can't figure it out, you can only believe it. Sovereignty is a scriptural fact!"
Faith is the only way you and I can please God, even when dealing with the seeming paradox between sovereignty and free will. (See Hebrews 11:6)

Obey every man-made authority for the Lord's sake – whether it is
the emperor, as the supreme ruler, or the governors whom he has
appointed to punish evil-doers and reward those who do good ser-
vice. It is the will of God that you may thus silence the ill-informed
criticisms of the foolish. As free men you should never use your

---

7 Ravi Zacharias International Ministries podcast, Nov. 15, 2017. Copyright RZIM.

freedom as an excuse for doing something that is wrong, for you are at all times the servants of God. You should have respect for everyone, you should love our brotherhood, fear God and honour the emperor.
1 Peter 2:13-17 Phillips

How Can I Trust a Sovereign God?

There is nothing – no circumstance, no trouble, no testing – that can ever touch me until, first of all, it has gone past God and past Christ right through to me.

Alan Redpath
British evangelist, pastor, and author
1907 - 1989

God did this so that they would seek Him and perhaps reach out for Him and find Him, though He is not far from any one of us.
Acts 17:27 NIV

My Opinions are Imprisoning

Inevitably God's sovereignty is an issue of the heart and a battle fought in the mind. Our resistance to God's sovereignty is rooted in our unworthy thoughts and opinions stemming from our rebellious hearts. Resistance is playing God and claiming His throne as our own. From this position we dictate what we think is right or wrong. If I tell the Lord how He should operate, do you think I will have any qualms in telling you how you should operate, as well?

But such a position is a prison! We imprison ourselves and those around us by holding to our judgments. Acceptance of God's sovereignty, on the other hand, liberates us and frees us to live in a heavenly realm. It is only when we expose these erroneous thoughts that we can live in the comfort and security of God's sovereign hands.

Our opinions wall us in and restricts our acceptance of God's sovereign move in our lives. We maintain these deadly judgments enforcing them as LAW. I have met so many people who defend their opinions, evangelize for them, and enact punitive judgments on anyone who dissents. It is death!

We exhaust too much energy in building and defending our opinions and judgments. We place our passion and the force of our energy behind them. They are laws after all; we feel we must enforce their rightness against those who would resist them.

I recently heard of a man who went on a tirade because his neighbors were not using their porch! He raved on and on about how they were wasting that space, as it if were a capital offense. As far as he was concerned, he knew best and they were wrong. They should follow the law of his judgment, even with their own property. What did it matter that the property did not belong to him?

I wish this type of behavior was uncommon, but we are all legalists to varying degrees. "He should have...!" "Why didn't she...?" "It would have been better if...!" Each is playing God.

Amazingly, we find it easy to have opinions about anything, from the minuscule ("They waste a lot of time watching sports") to the major ("They can't even take care of the children they have; they should have stopped after two!") I could tell you how best to pump gas or when you should put on your turn signal. And I do not even need to remain within my area of knowledge and expertise. My opinions spill over into every arena of life!

The sad truth is, judgment is death, the death of trying to be God. I am no one's Holy Spirit. The Spirit of God alone maintains that right in every life. I will not be the one answering for your choices, unless I have direct authority in your life. What I am talking about here is not the responsibility of authority, but the random assaults my opinions launch on those who do not answer to me.

These intrusive opinions are a deadly parting gift from our Fall in the Garden of Eden. As a result of Adam and Eve's choice to disobey God by eating of the fruit of the Tree of the Knowledge of Good and Evil, we humans are under the delusion that we have the right to our judgments. And the same fruit that rotted inside of Adam and Eve continues to rot within us as we continue to pick and eat it.

Each of us has the option to choose: our opinion and judgment or the mind of Christ. It is either/or, not both. By enforcing our judgments, we prevent ourselves from seeing God's point of view. We imprison ourselves inside our sinful, humanly limiting views – and death.

Insisting on having our own opinions blinds us to God's sovereign move and to His amazing workings in the lives of His creatures. God knows we are but dust, and He is able to work together all things for the good of those who love Him (Romans 8:28).

We are simple sheep, so who can say if a foolish choice is not just a step toward God working out His salvation in that sheep's life? God orchestrates our lives knowing that we need His Shepherding, not in spite of that fact. If we receive Him as our all-encompassing Sovereign God, then we will have eyes to see His amazing power working miracles in the lives of other needy ones, just like us.

No soldier on service entangleth himself in the affairs of this life;
that he may please him who enrolled him as a soldier.
2 Timothy 2:4 ASV

Eating from the Tree of Knowledge

In the Garden of Eden, Adam and Eve were commanded *not* to eat from the Tree of Good and Evil (Tree of Knowledge). The tree's fruit was poison and ingesting it would inevitably kill them, physically and spiritually. The will of the Lord set up a barrier against harm but the couple chose to eat the forbidden fruit regardless. They chose to listen to the slander of God spoken by the serpent, and believed the Lord was withholding from them the very thing they needed most— the need to know on their own. This was coupled with the lie that there would be no consequence for their sin of trying to meet their need independent of God.

Through this belief, they displaced God and in turn were displaced from God. They had a NEED to KNOW, and God was not telling them. More, He was maliciously withholding the *answer* to their need. This lie has been perpetuated in all of their children (us) to this very day.

Living by the Tree of the Knowledge of Good and Evil is a power that will turn on us, and turn in us. Eating this tree's fruits will make us sour and bitter toward God. He will become our assumed opponent, who is attacking and mis-treating us. And as a result, we will live resisting rather than receiving. We will live resisting everything from God that we consider evil and attempting to wrestle out of His hands things that we determine to be good. This is not Life: This is dancing with that serpent devil.

Everything in life will tempt us to return to the Tree of Knowledge. If we continue to eat that fruit, Satan wins and we will die. What's the alternative?

If we are not to live distinguishing between that which is

good and bad, then what is it we are supposed to do? It is simple, but not easy. The alternative is to live *listening*.

If we are eating the fruits of knowledge then we are involved in fixing what we believe God screwed up and manhandling Him to give us what is good – according to our judgment. We leave our relationship with Him and become entangled with the craziness instead. We become engaged in presuming and manipulating rather than simply pursuing Him.

I am going to tell on myself here giving you an instance of this in my life. I was following the US elections and as I watched, day by day, I saw continual blatant fraud and obstruction of justice. As a result, I got all twisted up. And when I get worked up, I tend to scour the world seeking answers to assuage my fears.

This time was no different. What was happening? I cried out. What are people doing to stop this? I raged. Taking this stance worked me into a lather of concern and fear.

Knowledge ever seeks more knowledge, ad nauseum. All this taking in of information, facts and figures does not alleviate my troubled soul. If anything, it only works me up more. The enemy always boasts of his power and prowess while magnifying my weakness. I become hopeless and discouraged, feeling as if all is lost.

I am not saying that knowledge is a bad thing; education gives us the skills to serve with excellence. Who would want an uneducated doctor, that is just a charlatan? What I am describing is the difference between seeking Truth rather than justifying our opinions. One comes in the humility of powerlessness and the other mounts a case to prove its rightness, regardless of facts.

The issue with this is simple; The Tree of Knowledge will *never* relieve my fears – it only increases them!

My answer is Christ, who is *The Answer*. When I turn to Him in prayer I have more power, more peace, more influence, and more Jesus. When will I ever learn that my greatest ability to influence any situation is not in gathering information but in seeking the heart of Jesus?

Refusing to eat from the Tree of Knowledge does not mean that I insulate and isolate myself in a soundproof safe room. I live and work in this world. I am going to be affected by what is going on around me. But refusing to eat from the Tree of Knowledge does mean that I must focus on my Source, Jesus, my Answer. Did I think that this was the first time in history that humans have conjured and cajoled to grasp power? Certainly not! Men and women of faith since the beginning have faced the antagonism of others and had to choose the Facts of God.

Look at the story of Nehemiah, found in the biblical Book of Nehemiah. In 586 B.C. this man was called by God to restore the wall of Jerusalem decimated when the Babylonians destroyed them. Once Nehemiah and his men were on site, they were harassed, mocked, criticized, lied about, threatened and attacked by men who answered to their opponents, Sanballat, Tobias and Geshem.

How did Nehemiah respond? He kept his eye on his task and listened to the Voice of God, not to inane reports of fear and rumors. The tsunami of "knowledge" coming against Nehemiah could have caused him to falter if he gave it credence. If he had engaged with the subterfuge of dissent, he could have lost it all.

What can we learn from Nehemiah? One thing is, we can maintain clarity and resolve. We cannot allow our reality to be defined by the chatter of "facts and figures" and the endless negative reports that swirl around us. Personally, I know I want to hear what the Voice of God is speaking to me! To hear His deeply intimate and personal Truth about each and every situation that concerns me.

Knowing God wants to speak to us, why is His Voice the last one many of us seek for truth? We have great influence in seeking the Lord and only feel powerless while listening to the endless negative reports. Instead we poll the world to see if we are safe, while Safety Himself dwells among us and within us. Our strength is in the Lord, and only in Him can we affect our world!

The LORD has looked down from heaven upon the sons of men to see if there are any who understand, who seek after God.
Psalm 14:2 NASB

For even though they knew God, they did not honor Him as God or give thanks, but they became futile in their speculations, and their foolish heart was darkened.
Romans 1:21 NASB

God did this so that they would seek Him and perhaps reach out for Him and find Him, though He is not far from any one of us.
Acts 17:27 NIV

If my people, who are called by my name, will humble themselves and pray and seek My face and turn from their wicked ways, then I will hear from heaven, and I will forgive their sin and will heal their land.
2 Chronicles 7:14 NIV

"But if I were you, I would appeal to God; I would lay my cause before Him. He performs wonders that cannot be fathomed, miracles that cannot be counted."
Job 5:8-9 NIV

But may all who seek You rejoice and be glad in You; may those who long for Your saving help always say, "The LORD is great!"
Psalm 40:16 NIV

Be Liberated from the Tree of Knowledge

Choosing to judge events by our fleshly standard of good and evil is living from the Tree of the Knowledge of Good and Evil. Deciding and dictating what we believe to be acceptable and unacceptable only produces death, confusion, and chaos.

Eating of the fruit of the Tree of the Knowledge of Good and Evil was the ruin of Adam and Eve, and it could be our ruin, as well. But when we choose to live our lives giving thanks to God, and trusting His sovereignty, we choose Life, thus liberating ourselves from the Tree of Knowledge.

Thanking God for everything sets us free. Men and women were never intended to live deciding and judging. No, we find our destiny in listening to the Voice of God. God intends us to give thanks to affirm what He has chosen for us.

"Shall we indeed accept [only] good from God and not [also] accept adversity and disaster?"
Job 2:10 AMP

Job's comment expresses a deeply Hebraic thought; Live in the mystery, open handedly receiving the whole of life from your Author who is God. Remember, Job was a contemporary of Abraham, so this type of thinking goes back thousands of years! I have discovered that this is a very difficult reality to accept, especially for those of us with a Western mindset. We feel safer in a singularly-sided reality (where things are either/or but not a paradox). When a seeming contradiction exists, we prefer to choose one side or the other, thus giving us the illusion of control. But living in the paradox of the contradiction allows *God to be God*.

When we live our lives making decisions about what is "good or bad," we are attempting to sit in the seat of the true Judge. This is not actual living at all!

God designed us to live life receiving all things – everything! – from His own hand. It is not up to us to decide what we will and will not accept from Him. When we live as judges, we live our lives close-fisted, grasping a gavel to club dissenters. Eating the fruit of the Tree of Knowledge makes us bitter and sour because we feel we have been wronged, misused and abused. These malicious fruits are delightful to our eyes, but once ingested, they prove deadly poisonous to our spirits and souls.

I am not promoting a Pollyanna existence where we live naive and stupid about the difficulties, evils and tough situations in our lives. Nor am I saying that we should lie down like doormats and let life plow us into the ground. It is true that not everything in our lives will feel good, but for the man or woman who seeks God, holding everything and everyone with an open hand, every circumstance in our lives will ultimately bless us. Yes, they will ultimately "work together for our good" (Romans 8:28).

Living a life where everything is cherry-flavored and sugarcoated is not brave, and it is NOT a life of faith! Courage is living by faith in God through Jesus Christ DESPITE the nitty-gritty, the awful, the sad, the disappointing events of our daily existence.

Life is to be lived in its entirety. Life is wholeness and fullness, not segregating and compartmentalizing. We cannot live only accepting the good, while rejecting the bad. The reality of the child of God is there is no good and bad, there's only *life.*

Anyone can live as an opinionated sorter and a judge: "This is right, this is wrong," or "This is good, this is bad." The truly courageous follower of Christ lives a life accepting, not rejecting, God's Sovereign Touch.

"Father, I abandon myself into Your hands; do with me what You will. Whatever You may do, I thank You; I am ready for all, I accept all.

"Let only Your will be done in me, and in all Your creatures – I wish no more than this, O Lord. Into Your hands I commend my soul: I offer it to You with all the love of my heart, for I love You, Lord, and so need to give myself; to surrender myself into Your hands without reserve and with boundless confidence, for You are my Father. Amen."

Charles de Foucauld
French Christian, explorer, Trappist monk
1858-1916

How is God Sovereign Over This World?

As truly as God by His power once created, so truly by that same power must God every moment maintain.

Andrew Murray
South African writer, teacher, and Christian pastor
1828 - 1917

God claims the world as His.
Everything and everyone belongs to Him!
Psalm 24:1 TPT

God is in Control: The World Unshaken

The Lord reigns! He is robed in majesty; The Lord is robed, enveloped in strength. The world is firmly established; it cannot be shaken.
Psalms 93:1 HCSB

"The world is firmly established; it cannot be shaken." I thought this phrase was strange the first time I read it, and "I asked the Lord what He meant by what He said." I knew that anything built and based on the world's standards is as unstable as shifting sand, so if the Lord says that the world is "firmly established," what does He mean?

I had to read it again. *"The world is firmly established; it cannot be shaken."* Aha! God was telling me that He is in control. **God is in control!** That gave me — and it should give you — tremendous hope!

God reigns on His throne *now*. Even though situations and circumstances tempt me to believe otherwise, the reality is that our Lord is reigning! Today!

God's sovereignty is *God rules – reigns – over everything.* God's reign establishes all things, and all things means everything!

From the Immeasurable...

Everything in this world has borders. The sea, the land, the nations, the sun, the moon – everything has limits. All things have borders that the Lord Himself establishes.
Even things as tiny as a leaf or a drop of rain or a grain of sand have edges that limit the space they are allowed to cover, and not any more. When I was driving to the office

one day, I saw the edges of everything. From the road to the mountains, the trees to the leaves, all had lines set by the Creator who rules. This brought me enormous peace. Even if I do not like the bounds, limits, and restrictions of any given thing, they still exist. He still is over all. Even my very own body is contained by His limits.

Nothing is allowed to run haphazardly in the Lord's creation: Everything in every way has constraints. Nothing extends beyond His reach nor exceeds His limitation.

Understanding God's established borders offers us the reassuring yet frightening fact that nothing moves beyond its limited, given space. Nothing.

Naturally, this understanding also unleashes a whole array of issues. "God, You could have limited that. Why didn't You?" When we ask this very common, human question, we are wrestling with His sovereignty.

A WORLD IN HIS HANDS

While I was writing these thoughts, Martha Kilpatrick happened by and commented, "If we really knew the Father's sufficiency, His commitment and His presence, then we would be content no matter what the situation. And not only content, but in ecstasy."

Wow! Couple that with this quote from one of Martha's devotional thoughts on the word "Let": "There is never a problem outside of God's will and Jesus' dominion."[1]

---

1 Kilpatrick, Martha, LET Devotional Series, #33, "God's Perfect Order." ReadMK.com

I cannot manhandle God by forcing my way past His limitations. Yet I am safe within those very limitations because He is my Abba, my Daddy. I can live at peace in a world that is ruled by God's parameters and not just whirling about in seemingly chaotic happenstance. And if I will surrender to His rule, as Martha said, I will find not only contentment – I will find ecstasy.

The Earth is the Lord's...

*The earth is the Lord's, and the fullness thereof; the world, and
they that dwell therein.*
Psalms 24:1 KJV

Would I allow someone to come into my house and tell me
what to do? Where to hang my pictures? Where to place my
bed? How to arrange my tools? No, of course not.

In the same way, this world is God's, and it will be run just
as He wants it to be run.

I admit that I have a list of objections to the way this world
is, to things I really wish were not as they are. Some facts
and realities about this world seem immovable, causing me
great pain. Yet I have little influence over them, or ability to
change them. I might writhe and twist and complain, but
they move not one iota. They simply are, and they are in
God's world as He has made it.

God does what He wants with His Creation – because it is
His Creation! I live here as a guest, not an owner.

You will notice that people attempting to escape account-
ability through atheism usually say, "How could a loving
God allow all the pain and suffering that exist in this world?
Now, this question may come out of genuinely painful mem-
ories or an attempt to avoid God's wooing call on their life.
But ultimately it arises from an underlying accusation, "God,
you're a failure! A good God wouldn't allow suffering. Actually, I could do it better!"

Like all humanity, I, too, used to believe that I had the right
to place my dissatisfied comments about God's world in the

Suggestion Box. I wanted to get rid of all abuse, change the things I did not like about my parents or family, feed the world, save the babies, eradicate this or that evil, change my own history, and establish world peace — the list goes on and on in HIS WORLD. I wondered why God did not make humans submissive rather than capable of rebellion. Or why He required His Son to be brutally murdered on a cross to pay for our rebellion.

But this is God's world, and each time I began my litany of complaints I came back to a basic truth: The Ways of God are always perfect, and perfect for me. I might not understand them or like them – but they are still perfect. This is God's house, and He does things according to His pleasure, not mine.

I AM God, and there is no other; I AM God, and there is none like Me.
Isaiah 46:9 HCSB

Worshiping the Ways of God is a huge work of the Spirit. Submitting to His complete sovereignty happens as we see Him and know that He alone is God. To know God's Ways is to know Him, and to receive His Ways is to receive Him. No matter how our egos might deceive us, the earth is the Lord's, and the fullness thereof.

No matter how our egos might deceive us, the earth is the Lord's, and the fullness thereof.

To know God's Ways is to know Him,
and to receive His Ways is to receive Him.

You will keep in perfect peace all who trust in You, all whose thoughts are fixed on You!
Isaiah 26:3 NLT

All Creation is Calling

I have always been amazed by what all of Creation – the totality of Creation – teaches us. God created the Heavens and the Earth and all that lives. At the end of His work of creating this masterpiece of the world and universe in which we live, He blessed it, saying, "It is very good."
Then came man, made in God's image. We roamed the earth and were given preeminence over all Creation. We were able to walk in the cool of the day with God, our Father, in unbroken fellowship. It was beautiful!

Until the day that we fell.

As a result of our choice to disobey God, all of Creation then and for all the generations to come was cursed—not by God, but by sin. Fruitfulness and flourishing gave way to thorns and thistles. On that day, death and decay permeated everything God had created. All that had been blessed and declared VERY good bore the scars of humanity's rebellion against God.

Did Creation turn against us in revulsion and bitterness? Did the Earth swallow us whole in revenge for mangling its form? No, the Word says instead that all Creation longs for the sons of God to come into glory – to return to full relationship with Him. Creation literally groans as it waits to see us reunited with God in perfection.

For the creation eagerly waits with anticipation for God's sons to be revealed.
Romans 8:19 HCSB

Everything on earth was subject to our rebellion, our fall from perfect communion with God. Nature itself was marred by our evil choice, and yet lives in hope and anticipation. Imagine! Hope reigns supreme throughout all Creation even in the face of our ongoing evil. Creation teems with expectation for the day when we – and it – will be liberated, restored, renewed.

For the creation was subjected to futility – not willingly, but because of Him who subjected it – in the hope that the creation itself will also be set free from the bondage of corruption into the glorious freedom of God's children. For we know that the whole creation has been groaning together with labor pains until now.
Romans 8:20-22 HCSB

How does this relate to us today? The Creation Story is the same in the microcosm as it is in the macrocosm. It is reflected in our personal lives as well. In the same way that Creation was hurt by our choices, other people's choices have and do hurt us deeply. Creation teaches us how to bow to God's sovereignty in suffering for the higher purpose: the Will of God.

Whether through ignorance, willfulness, or with malice, we are wounded, scarred, even crippled by the choices of those around us. Parents or siblings, spouses or children, authorities or friends wound us, sometimes irrevocably. And we wound others as much as they wound us.

But here is Creation standing as an ever-present sentinel, a beacon of hope, demonstrating how it bowed to the Sovereign Hand that subjected it to mankind. Now Creation groans and waits for the redemption we all seek. Which one of us has not also had to twist in the wind of adversity, waiting for our Redeemer in Glory to deliver us?

The reality of our bowing, of our groaning, of our waiting

could sink us emotionally if we did not have the sustaining power of the Spirit of God to "help us in our weakness" (Romans 8:26). Without Him it is impossible, unsustainable, devastating – too much to bear on our own. The good news is that we were never intended to bear it alone.

Our Savior died on the Cross to heal the breach, and He left the Spirit to live within us on a 24/7/365 basis. The story of His Redeeming Love is sung throughout Creation. All Creation calls, waiting patiently without bitterness, malice or scorn.

This is our lesson and our life. We are each called to receive our bruising, accept our crippling, and groan with all Creation for the Redemption that will come at the end of the age.

Am I a pessimist? A gloomy Gus sporting a "Life's a bummer and then you die!" bumper sticker? On the contrary, I know that God has subjected me to, and I have been maligned by, the choices of others. I am called to embrace His sovereign choices and not to take up bitterness against those who have sinned against me. In addition, others are the recipients of my own sinful choosing; may they have the grace to embrace our Sovereign God and forgive me as well.

All Creation has a lesson to teach us: Surrender to the Hand of our Sovereign God and eagerly wait, groaning at times, for His Sovereign Hand to liberate us all. Oh, how often I have been offended in this process, and become bitter, writhing with resistance rather than groaning with anticipation.

It is a life or death choice. God has given each of us His grace to face it.

In my opinion whatever we may have to go through now is less than nothing compared with the magnificent future God has planned for us. The whole creation is on tiptoe to see the wonderful sight of the sons of God coming into their own. The world of creation cannot as yet see reality, not because it chooses to be blind, but because in God's purpose it has been so limited – yet it has been given hope. And the hope is that in the end the whole of created life will be rescued from the tyranny of change and decay, and have its share in that magnificent liberty which can only belong to the children of God!

Romans 8:18-21 Phillips

Me and the Milky Way

The Earth is perfectly positioned for optimum viewing of
God's expansive Creation, as well as for maintaining the del-
icate balance to sustain life in all its forms. The Milky Way
is an incomprehensible 100,000 light years across, and the
Earth sits in its slim "galactic habitable zone" just far enough
from the center that we are not killed by radiation, and just
close enough to the center that the heavy elements needed
for life are present. Amazingly this position is also a perfect
seat for viewing the rest of the cosmos.

"For some reason our earthly location is extraordinarily
well suited to allow us to peer into the heavens and discover
its secrets," say the grateful astronomers who authored *The
Privileged Planet*.[2]

In the same way, each human being rests perfectly secure in
the palm of God's life-sustaining hand. And each of us is positioned in our lives so that we can perfectly witness God's
divine orchestration of our days, weeks and years. As we do,
we increasingly come to know Him and to love Him.

Neither you nor I is one millimeter out of His handpicked
spot for us to dwell, both universally and individually. Our
God is perfectly sovereign over all our lives and each of us
must grapple with the reality of that sovereignty. The question we all ask can follow us throughout our lives: "Is God
absolutely sovereign over every aspect of our lives?" If the
answer is "No," then He is not sovereign at all. Each of us
must make peace with this reality. Your life and mine are

---

2 Gonzalez, Guillermo, and Richards, Jay W., THE PRIVILEGED PLAN-
ET: How Our Place in the Cosmos is Designed for Discovery. Regnery
Publishing Inc., Washington, D.C. Copyright 2003.

perfectly orchestrated, painful situations and all, so that we can discover God and receive all that He has for us.

From Large to Small...

Truly, God's sovereignty reigns in amazing and mysterious ways over every massive planet, every black hole in the sky, every beach the oceans on earth touch, every glacier that carves, down to every nook and cranny of the entire universe. But His Sovereign Touch also reaches to the "days of our lives," to our circumstances and experiences, to our choices, good and bad, to the wonderful and awful events that shape us, and to the choices other people make, as well.

Truly God is completely sovereign, from the minuscule to the magnanimous. The Sovereign Touch knows no bounds and reaches far and wide into our very lives. None of us remain unaffected and those who embrace His reality are enviable and endlessly blessed.

Receiving the Sovereign Touch

Men will allow God to be everywhere but on His throne.... When God ascends His throne, His creatures then gnash their teeth....

Charles Haddon Spurgeon
English Particular Baptist preacher
1834 – 1892

He existed before anything was made,
and now everything finds completion in Him.
Colossians 1:17 TPT

The Key to Accepting Sovereignty

If you want to know if you have truly accepted God's sovereignty, go watch the news for a few minutes and see if your blood pressure rises. This is not the only place we struggle with sovereignty, of course, but for me it is a real quick barometer! Why? Because if our God is sovereign, and no man holds office unless it is God's Will, then I have to do a great work of surrender as I watch our elected officials do the most ungodly things.

God's sovereignty is one of those subjects that has troubled every human being throughout history. It is a reality that only a spiritual man or woman can truly receive and accept. Sovereignty is about the absolute Lordship of Jesus Christ. And the key to accepting His Lordship is the same key that liberated us from the Tree of Knowledge: We must learn to give thanks to God in all things. (See 1 Thessalonians 5:18)

This key does not open the door without a concerted effort, however, and that effort involves a deliberate choice. This is some of the hardest spiritual work we will ever have to do, perhaps right up there with forgiveness – and you know as well as I do that forgiveness is hard! Embracing God's sovereignty is more than hard: It encompasses all of life, and it is where the rubber meets the road. As I said before, God is either sovereign over all or He is not sovereign at all!

But on the other side of this great work, we will experience true hope, joy and contentment.

EVERYTHING MEANS EVERYTHING

When I speak of giving thanks as the key that opens the door to accepting God's sovereignty, I am not talking about general gratitude, like thanking God for a spouse, for children, for a job, or for a beautiful sunset. I am speaking of a specific issuing of thanks in the midst of a specific situation. Like the passing of Martha's daughter-in-law in the car accident? Martha gave an "offering of thanks," which forwent feelings or understanding. She presented gratitude as a gift to Him, because He is her sovereign. This transaction also took the control out of her hands and place the situation solely into His.

How do we respond, for instance, when a political candidate whose policies we strongly oppose wins a hotly contested legislative seat, throwing our state into chaos? Thanking God for that win, which crosses our will, is not an easy choice. In addition, thanking God for things that have wounded us deeply, things we see as negative and cruel, which have fundamentally affected our lives is equally as tough. But look at what the Scriptures say:

Be thankful, whatever the circumstances may be. If you follow this advice you will be working out the will of God expressed to you in Jesus Christ.
1 Thessalonians 5:18 Phillips

Most of us have at least one single event or hurtful relationship that has fundamentally and radically affected our lives, that has altered our core in a dramatic way. Christ Himself experienced not only the normal gamut of troubling difficulties in His life – but He also suffered a horrendously painful and torturous death!

Is God asking us to thank Him for even our most painful, life-altering events and situations? Are we to thank Him for the very things that tempt me to stop trusting and leave me with an emotional limp?

The reason God wants us to thank Him for everything is because this is the way to access His abundant Life, where everything becomes our blessing. God is not wringing His hands and saying, "Thank ME for everything, especially those things that hurt you, muwah ha ha ha!" Rather He is saying, "Thank ME for everything because I want to bless you!"

There is an art to being grateful, and the lack of it is the end of life. Romans 1:21-32 tells us that there is a downward spiral of degradation for any who fail to be grateful.

For although they knew God, they did not honor Him as God or give thanks to Him, but they became futile in their thinking, and their foolish hearts were darkened. Claiming to be wise, they became fools, and exchanged the glory of the immortal God for images resembling mortal man and birds and animals and creeping things.

Therefore God gave them over in the sinful desires of their hearts to sexual impurity for the degrading of their bodies with one another. They exchanged the truth about God for a lie, and worshiped and served created things rather than the Creator — who is forever praised. Amen.

Because of this, God gave them over to shameful lusts. Even their women exchanged natural sexual relations for unnatural ones. In the same way the men also abandoned natural relations with women and were inflamed with lust for one another. Men committed shameful acts with other men, and received in themselves the due penalty for their error.

Furthermore, just as they did not think it worthwhile to retain the knowledge of God, so God gave them over to a depraved mind, so

that they do what ought not to be done. They have become filled with every kind of wickedness, evil, greed and depravity. They are full of envy, murder, strife, deceit and malice. They are gossips, slanderers, God-haters, insolent, arrogant and boastful; they invent ways of doing evil; they disobey their parents; they have no understanding, no fidelity, no love, no mercy. Although they know God's righteous decree that those who do such things deserve death, they not only continue to do these very things but also approve of those who practice them.
Romans 1:21-32 ESV

The above passages make clear that this downward spiral, this entropy, leads to terrible repercussions that demonstrate in every kind of immorality and soul sickness. Verses 21-31 list unrighteousness of all kinds; pride; greed; malice; sexual immorality; homosexual acts; envy; covetousness; rivalry; treachery; haughtiness; strive; deceit; evil-mindedness; disrespect of parents; faithlessness; murder; spitefulness; gossip; insolence and reviling; boastfulness; senselessness; heartlessness; ruthlessness; violence; backbiting; invention of evil; lack of discernment; lack of trustworthiness; lack of love; lack of forgiveness; lack of mercy; hatred of God.

Amazing – this sounds exactly like what we are seeing so clearly in our society! And it is a high price to pay for the "privilege" or stubborn refusal to withhold gratitude! I cannot say that I have not danced all over this list, myself, when I have refused to honor our God as GOD, resisting His call to be grateful.

God's design for our life on earth is that we would be blessed regardless of our circumstances, but thanksgiving is the door to receiving those blessings.

I have learned, often in the most painful ways, that God

actually does "work all things together for good for those who love Him and are called according to His purpose." This includes the hurtful situations that have marked me. Remember what I said earlier? God weaves the fabric of our lives, includes some very painful threads, to weave a tapestry more amazing than we could ever know. Again, God is either totally sovereign, or not sovereign at all.

It always comes down to this: God's sovereignty over our lives. Can we trust God's sovereign hand and His character in our life dealings? Yes, because when we come to the place of thanking Him for those painful events, situations or relationships, He reveals to us His purposes and plans in them. And here is the weirdest part of this spiritual work: These painful wounds become blessings in themselves. What we once labeled curses God uncovers as part of His actual blessing!

In my own life, I can look back and see that painful, negative, soul-crushing events have been exposed as my biggest blessings! Aside from God, isolated in a void of God's presence and action, no one would celebrate the memory of these circumstances. But today they stand as beacons of blessing through which the Lord has flooded my life with treasure.

Each person must walk their path alone with the Lord. No one can tell us that an abuse is a blessing until God has revealed it.

The secret blessing of suffering is only revealed to those who take the first step and thank God for it.

Giving thanks for bad and painful circumstances may sound odd. "Why in the world would I be grateful for things that appear detrimental and hurtful?" we ask. The answer is that

every circumstance contains blessing for the child of God.
If I give thanks, it is impossible for me to be His and not
be blessed by His hands in all of my circumstances. Giving
thanks, again, is the key that opens the door to God's blessing. Conversely, ingratitude shuts the door.

In this fallen world, God takes shocking measures to bring
us into glorious, abundant Life (see John 10:10). Crushing
circumstances crack our pride, hurtful situations expose our
raw need, and penetrating pains ignite our motivation to
seek help. *To seek God.*

At the end of the day, we can choose one of two attitudes for
dealing with our suffering: bitterness or thankfulness. We
can let the pain fester and make us toxic, or we can thank the
Father and let Him bring forth Life. The choice is ever before
us: life or death, blessing or curse (see Deuteronomy 11:26).

*And give thanks for everything to God the Father in the name of
our Lord Jesus Christ.*
Ephesians 5:20 NLT

The first step is the obedient choice to thank Him. At the beginning, it is only *a choice*, and it may sound something like
this: "Thank You, Father, that You are God. Thank You that
You are sovereign. Thank You that You truly can work all
things together for the good of those who love You and are
called according to Your purpose. Thank You that You care
more about my eternal destiny than about my momentary
opposition and complaints. Thank You that I can trust You
with my life, even in my pain."

From that point on (and you will find yourself needing to repeat this prayer often, as pain, by nature, attacks relentlessly)
it is God's business "to will and to do of His good pleasure"

(Phil. 2:13). When we obediently thank Him, even without understanding the hows and whys, He meets us at our point of choice and floods us, in His own perfect time, with acceptance, revelation, and understanding. Eventually we see His hand at work and how our suffering was used in our life (and often in the lives of others.) We will be amazed as we watch God turn what we called a curse into a blessing.

GIVING THANKS IS NOT ALWAYS EASY

To be clear, I am not talking about giving thanks with glee. I am not saying we will feel overwhelming joy as we make this choice. I am saying that we must exercise thanksgiving as an act of surrender and worship.

Giving thanks for the things we do not like, proclaims Jesus Christ is Lord. Thanks determines I will believe that He is my sovereign Lord. There is no more powerful proclamation to our souls than this: "No matter what the circumstances look like, I will believe in God who is on the Throne of Heaven and Earth!"

This is the gratitude that opens the door to accepting and embracing God's sovereignty. True hope, joy and contentment will follow.

More often than not, spiritual growth ends at the point where we refuse to believe or accept the sovereignty of God. If we declare that God is not sovereign in a particular area of our lives, then we are saying He is not Lord. And if God is not Lord, He is not OUR Lord. This is a life or death issue: Being willing to thank God for everything is the key.

We live in torment when we do not believe that God is sovereign. We are vulnerable to the world's chaos and we are, quite frankly, not safe. Talk about scaring sheep! It is frightening when we are left hanging in the wind, our peace destroyed.

Thanking God for all things, though, proclaims His Lordship to our world. It is a choice to trust Him, because He is trustworthy. Rather than saving ourselves and losing our lives, giving thanks empowers us to abandon ourselves and find our lives! (See Luke 9:24 and Luke 17:33.)

There is no greater contentment than to know we are safe in the hands of an All-powerful God. We may not have understanding in the moment of crisis, but when we know our destiny is intact, we have hope. We also have joy and peace in knowing that Jesus rules over all, even the evil of man.

In one of his booklets, R.C. Sprouts says, "The more we understand God's sovereignty, the more our prayers will be filled with thanksgiving."[1]

---

1 R.C. Sproul's Crucial Questions booklet Does Prayer Change Things?, Reformation Trust Publishing.

What is the Purpose of Prayer?

Another friend asked me, "If God is sovereign, then what is the purpose of prayer?" Great question! And I believe I have an answer, but it is multi-faceted, so let me peel it down.

First, let me get something out of the way. Here is what sovereignty is NOT: It is not a parent saying, "Because I say so!" Sovereignty is not a power struggle or a punishment. It is an invitation to enter into God's place of safety. Our Heavenly Father is not an earthly parent with human motivations. If you view God's sovereignty with an assumption of His anger, nothing I have written will make sense.

A quick reminder: God's sovereignty over all things does not release me from responsibility. Just because God knows what the outcome will be – and everything happens by His sovereign Hand – does not mean that I can just lie back and let it happen. God has roles for me to play in the outworking of His Kingdom. I can exercise my free will, refuse to obey, and miss out on His glorious victories. Or I can agree with His plan and be a participant in the outcome!

So why pray? Prayer in the face of God's sovereignty affects me more than anything. Fervent prayer is deeply humbling, as well as character building. Fervent prayer has the potential to change ME. In the wrestling, I come to the mat where I can be refined, where the choices of my life can be defined. If I do not know where I am—in my attitudes, will, perspective, etc. – before praying, I certainly will after having to wait for an answer.

Fervent prayer is also relational, purposed to perpetuate my relationship with the Three Persons of the Godhead.

Prayer isn't to get my way, it's to know The Way.

Prayer is entwined with God's sovereignty so that I can know the Person of Christ who is The Way, The Truth, and The Life.

You see, like most earthly fathers, our Heavenly Father wants interaction and communion with His children. Fervent prayer is open communication – open conversation – with our Father. It involves seeking Him, His face and His fellowship.

Sure, if I am fervently praying for something, I am usually looking for the answer to my prayer more than anything else. I want a supply in some arena of my life. But while I may be singularly focused on an answer, God's aim is that I develop a deeper knowledge of Christ.

Does fervent prayer move the heart of the King? Yes! Our petitions can affect the outcome of a situation.

You and I are not praying to a lifeless statue: We are seeking our living Jesus, who has compassion on us and sympathizes with our weakness, for He faced the same kind of testing we do. Prayer is not directed to a stoic entity, His sovereignty knows the Answer.

Look at the Canaanite woman who did not care how humiliated she would be by her insistent prayer; she had to have His Answer. Jesus was THE healer and deliverer and He HAD to do so for her own daughter. Jesus was even insulting to her, stating the Jewish view of the Canaanites, but she did not defend or become angry. He just HAD to heal her daughter. Oh how He loved this!

But Jesus replied, "It is not right to take the children's bread and toss it to the dogs." "Yes, Lord," she said, "even the dogs eat the crumbs that fall from their master's table." Then Jesus replied to her, "Woman, your faith is great. Let it be done for you as you want." And from that moment her daughter was cured.
Matthew 15:26-28 HCSB

Jesus commended her faith – not her prayer, not her will, not her volume, but her faith. She connected her faith to her desperation and shameless persistence. And in response to her faith, Jesus joyfully answered.

ANOTHER REASON TO PRAY

Are you still looking for another reason to pray? Here is one: God asked us to do it!

Rejoice always, pray without ceasing, give thanks in all circumstances; for this is the will of God in Christ Jesus for you.
1 Thessalonians 5:16-18 ESV

God asks us to pray, and there are deep reasons why. One of them is for us to become His Bride.

Prayer is bridal and intended to be deeply intimate. Again the Hebrew word for the intimate knowing of marital union is yada. Think about discussions you have had with your spouse about life. I am talking about moments of heart revelation, not just common interaction. That kind of communication is as intimate as being deeply known in the physical sense. This is what prayer is for us.

Do I take this too far? Probably not far enough! The landscape of the Christian's world is for *knowing* our Beloved, Jesus. So how could prayer, discussions and supplications be for anything less than love?

In this matter of prayer, God's Lordship is never in question, but He desires our participation and agreement. Jesus is Lord but His plan is for us to co-reign with Him. Our participation is not an exercise in futility or endurance. It is all about love — His love for us, and our love for Him.
Prayer is not about arm-twisting or a needy man's plea. It is all about union life with our Beloved.

I know that in our task-oriented, performance-driven world, relegating prayer to the realm of love seems counterproductive. But apart from Love – God – we can do nothing! (See John 15.) Yes, answered prayer is important, but it is more important to know the Answerer.

Bowing to God's sovereignty in this matter of prayer is a surrender to His Lordship. It is an affirmative statement that we are on the right team, and that our Commander holds our complete destiny.

Circling back to our original question: If God is sovereign, what is the purpose of prayer?

The purpose is multifaceted, just as I said: 1) we are being changed through the process of prayer; 2) we are coming into deeper relationship with God through communion; and 3) we are being prepared as His Bride so that we may reign with the King of Glory.

The motivation for prayer is LOVE. I do not pray to manipulate God; I pray to fellowship with God. I come to know Him through prayer and I am known, myself. Prayer is a deeply revealing mirror exposing my heart and soul while presenting me with opportunities for transformation.

Prayer changes me, even as God's sovereignty holds me.

If I speak with the eloquence of men and of angels, but have no love, I become no more than blaring brass or crashing cymbal. If I have the gift of foretelling the future and hold in my mind not only all human knowledge but the very secrets of God, and if I also have that absolute faith which can move mountains, but have no love, I amount to nothing at all. If I dispose of all that I possess, yes, even if I give my own body to be burned, but have no love, I achieve precisely nothing.
1 Corinthians 13:1-3 Philips

THE SOVEREIGN END

Locked within the core of our lives, beneath all the happenings both what we would call good and bad, is a secret preparation beyond what most can even fathom. Truly, everything in this life is purposed, nothing is in vain. We are being prepared for a high calling and plan, which has a Reward beyond comparison.

In my opinion whatever we may have to go through now is less than nothing compared with the magnificent future God has planned for us.
Romans 8:18 Phillips

We are called to be the Bride of Christ, which alone is awe inspiring! An eternal union with our Kinsman Redeemer. WOW! But our union with Christ has another deep eternal purpose and plan—to rule and reign with Him as King forever. Our position is for co-reigning with the Eternal King. This makes all the trials we go through now more than just something we have to endure or overcome, it is about training for reigning.

The Will of God is for us to reign with Christ. All of life invites us to answer this call and we do this by bowing to His Lordship and receiving His Sovereign Touch. Reigning with Him is the eternal reward for being an overcomer. Those who live in the Will of God are being trained to rule and reign with Christ for the Eternal Kingdom.

I rely on this saying: If we died with Him we shall also live with Him: if we suffer with Him we shall also reign with Him.
2 Timothy 2:11-12 Phillips

And you have caused them to become a Kingdom of priests for our God. And they will reign on the earth.
Revelations 5:10 NLT

Imagine, from the momentary to the life-long, all events are the training ground preparing us to reign. We are in the school of preparation for an eternal position with Christ. It is in our daily lives where we receive this training.

This life is a training field to test our resolve. The question, will we surrender to His sovereignty and abandon our hearts to Him or will we resist His rule and reserve our lives? Those who yield in this life to His Lordship will reign in eternity. It is so crucial.

Our King will not sit on His throne with a rebel bride. The resistant to Him in this life will not be rewarded by reigning with Him in the next. How could Christ reign with one who refused to be ruled now? His Bride will be ONE in mind and Will with Him. Co-reigning means perfect union, equally yoked, with no division.

Do you see why it is so crucial that we embrace His Sovereign Will now? Our lives will prove our internal choices, whether we said yes or no to Him as Sovereign LORD. The consequence of receiving His Sovereign Touch now is our eternal elevation and Reward. Our choice to know Him as Sovereign will be met with Great Knowledge of Him.

On the other hand, our refusal to let Him be Lord over us now will be met with a devastating outcome. Our true choice will be revealed through His response to us. Christ will say, 'Believe me, I never knew you!' We will not be known because we would not know Him as Sovereign Lord. It just is not worth the cost on any front.

"At the time My coming draws near, heaven's kingdom realm can be compared to ten maidens who took their oil lamps and went outside to meet the bridegroom and his bride. Five of them were foolish and ill-prepared, for they took no extra oil for their lamps. Five of them were wise and sensible, for they took flasks of olive oil with their lamps.
When the bridegroom didn't come when they expected, they all grew drowsy and fell asleep. Then suddenly, in the middle of the night, they were awakened by the shout 'Get up! The bridegroom is here! Come out and have an encounter with him!' So all the girls got up and trimmed their lamps. But the foolish ones were running out of oil, so they said to the five wise ones, 'Share your oil with us, because our lamps are going out!'
"'We can't,' they replied. 'We don't have enough for all of us. You'll have to go and buy some for yourselves!'
"While the five girls were out buying oil, the bridegroom appeared. Those who were ready and waiting were escorted inside with him and the wedding party to enjoy the feast. And then the door was locked. Later, the five foolish girls came running up to the door and pleaded, 'Lord, Lord, let us come in!'
"But he called back, 'Go away! Do I know you? I can assure you, I don't even know you!'

That is the reason you should always stay awake and be alert, because you don't know the day or hour when the Bridegroom will appear."
Matthew 25:1-13 TPT

God's Pursuit of Us

We can never overestimate the often shocking lengths to which God will go in assisting us to know Him. He maneuvers and orchestrates situations so that He may be revealed. He is able to work situations together for this purpose. Our God is intense and passionate about wanting us to know Him!

Over and over again I have seen God orchestrate events in my life so that I have nothing but Him. At first glance, most of these happenings would not appear to be pleasant. I had always hoped for a Candy Land™ journey with gumdrop obstacles, but that has never been the case.

Which one of us could honestly say that blessing gets our attention more than difficulty? *All* of life – crises, troubles, pain, suffering and blessings, too – serves the sole purpose that all persons will come to Christ as His Bride and love Him as our Beloved. Sovereignty is *love*, not punishment or manhandling. It is deeply passionate *love*.

If you are currently in a crucible, know that it is for greater vision and an increased knowledge of your Lord. I have discovered, in fact, that the road to knowing God is fraught with more challenges than comfort.

My faith was tested through deep trials and with poignant crucibles. Juicing my finger off is one such example. I discovered that the road to knowing God is fraught with more challenges than comfort.

I say these words with all sincerity, not cynicism. And while I believe the statements above to be true, I would add that I do not believe God ever has any ill intent, or that He ever puts us through malicious hardship.

It just seems that we learn our lessons best through adversity rather than prosperity. Many of the fathers and mothers of our faith throughout the centuries concur. One of my favorites is by C.S. Lewis: "We can ignore even pleasure. But pain insists upon being attended to. God whispers to us in our pleasures, speaks in our conscience, but shouts in our pains: it is His megaphone to rouse a deaf world."[2]

But this section is not an analysis of why we might learn better through our crucibles. It is, instead, all about the greatness of our Father's pursuit of us, in order that He would be known by us. I am proclaiming that the God I have encountered again and again over my life's journey so desires to be known that He will do what it takes to reveal Himself, and to get my attention. The Bible says that "our God is a consuming fire" (Hebrews 12:29, KJV; see also Deuteronomy. 4:24 and 9:3, KJV). Our God is a consuming fire, which engulfs all that is not Him.

How far will our God go to make Himself known and to love us? He does whatever it takes, even to the point of crucifying His own Son. God created our world for His purpose and plan.

Though we "Adams and Eves" chose to spurn His ways in the Garden, our DNA vibrates toward Another's knowing. Even as we resist, God will make Himself known to His chosen.

---

2 The Problem of Pain by C.S. Lewis, Published by Harper One (first published 1940)

This is Just the Beginning

We are never going to embrace God's sovereignty on our
own. It simply is not in us to yield to The LORD over ALL.
WE can, as an act of our will, choose to say "yes" to His
Lordship, to give permission for Him to rule over us, and
this we must do. But the actual working out of that choice
must be done by Christ, through us. It is the Holy Spirit
of Christ Who will usher us into the Throne Room of God
being God over everything in our lives, including our most
difficult moments.

At the end of our days we will be able to claim only one
thing: Our God is God and He alone gets the glory for all, for
everything. I am not constructing a life to make God happy:
I am not capable of that. Jesus is forming His Life in me to
present to the Father.

It was nothing you could or did achieve — it was God's gift to you.
No one can pride himself upon earning the love of God. The fact is
that what we are we owe to the hand of God upon us.
Ephesians 2:8-9 Phillips

Each of us is working out our relationship with the Sovereign God, whether through our acceptance or rejection of
God as sovereign. And though today I might reject Him, He
is undaunted. Even in my trials, it is clear that Jesus is revealing Himself to me and opening my eyes to a greater seeing, a greater vision of Him. I love God for His willingness
to do what it takes. Life is not pain-free, but your interest
in exploring this subject with me causes me to believe that
yours is promised to experience the divine Union Life.

My highest prayer for everyone in these days is that we
would know – yada – the Lord our God in an ever-increas-

ing way. Whatever our tests and trials, may we see Him Who has redeemed us and purchased our ability to deeply *know* Him. And may we use the key of gratitude to open the door to this, His highest blessing!

Knowing God as Sovereign Lord
— Epilogue —

I have been asked hundreds of times in my life why God allows tragedy and suffering. I have to confess that I really do not know the answer totally, even to my own satisfaction. I have to accept, by faith, that God is sovereign, and He is a God of love and mercy and compassion in the midst of suffering.

Billy Graham
Southern Baptist minister, internationally known evangelist, author, and founder of the Billy Graham Evangelistic Association
1918 - 2018

And He chose us to be His very own, joining us to Himself even before He laid the foundation of the universe! Because of His great love, He ordained us, so that we would be seen as holy in His eyes with an unstained innocence.
Ephesian 1:4 TPT

The Urgency of Accepting God's Sovereignty

Why is it so urgent that we come to accept God's sovereignty? Why can't I just live my life accepting blessings from God and believing the devil is at work in my hardships? As I have shown, the repercussions of refusing to receive a sovereign God over all our lives are huge!

We quite often find ourselves pondering the issue of God's sovereignty when we are dealing with life events we don't like. We usually have no difficulty believing God is and was sovereign over our blessings. That is not in contention.

No, our wrestling is about those times when we have felt God was not in control of our lives. And while we might paint a religious facade on our actions, the result of not receiving God as God and giving Him thanks is utter degradation.

As believers, we are required, not requested, to honor God as sovereign Author of our lives, and to thank Him for ALL of it. He chose each of our stories and He is going to use ALL things to bring about His glorification and our growth in the knowledge of Him. ALL things. I am not being heavy handed in this; it is just that dire.

The Reason and Result

All of life is about relationships. All of us will have relationships with someone, or several someones, or something or
things.

Ultimately, though, life is about ONE relationship: We are
here to get acquainted with our sovereign Author. Sovereignty is not about God browbeating us into submission. It
is about His revealing to us the Son of God in all His glory
– the Son of God Whose deep desire is to be in relationship
with us.

If the Lord of life, Author of ALL happenings, wishes to
make Himself known in all our moments, who are we to
resist? Do we tell Him where we will acknowledge Him, and
where we will not? Do we relegate Him only to our happy
moments or the things we enjoy in this life?

That is not living – that is attempting to be God! Life is pain
as well as happiness, sorrow as well as ecstasy. We are on
this earth to know Him, to know the God who created us to
function and thrive in this world. Additionally, we are called
to be witnesses to Him in ALL circumstances.

Here is our choice: Do we want relationship with Him or
mere interaction with our pain? If we choose to engage only
with our wounds, our pain, and our suffering, we will lose
the potential for an astounding relationship with God because of our bitterness.

In writing this book, I am not insinuating that I am one who
has dealt with God's sovereignty over my life in a way that
is anywhere near perfect! On the contrary, for most of my life
I have related to God's sovereignty in ways that were hor-

ribly wrong! My coming to know a sovereign God was not pretty or gracious. Most of my early years sounded more like a pig farm on slaughter day. It was gruesome, just like everyone else's story throughout all of human history!

But as I came to see God as my rightful Owner, I entered into the peace of experiencing Him in ALL of life. And this is part of my sovereign story. No one gets the Miss Congeniality award in this process. We are talking about real pain, real suffering, and real human life. Yet this life is a one-time shot, and that is why we must choose rightly in relation to God's sovereignty. Am I waving my "right to a happy life done my way" in God's face? If so, I will miss the point of life and God's intent behind every event I experience.

Accepting God's Sovereign Touch in my life does not allow me to bypass difficulty or pain. Instead, it assures me that I will experience ALL of life with God, and that what I experience will be HIS Life, His abundant Life. Pain will still come. Tragedies will still befall me. But Christ will be at the center of my existence, and He will work ALL things together for good because I love Him.

Entrusted for Worship

Deliver to the God of Jerusalem all the articles entrusted to you for worship in the temple of your God.
Ezra 7:19 NIV

God has entrusted each of us with articles intended to worship Him. What are they? You may be shocked, as they do not rank on any standard Christian chart. I believe that our life crises and painful situations are intended to be brought forth as pure gold and silver vessels with which we can worship God. Now I will show you the living reality which goes beyond the gold and silver items used in churches and temples. I want to show you the human elements forged for worship.

Let me tell you about my friend Josh. His raw, encrusted element of God's choosing was the heartbreaking abuse from a sibling. As a young man he was relentlessly harassed and physically assaulted by his older brother. This started in his childhood and continued into his young adulthood. I do not make light of his pain, but as he has discovered and testified to me, God used his pain for good.

My question, how could this abuse be an entrusted element of worship? It was painful and abusive for sure, but did God entrust this man with it for a higher purpose – the worship of the High King of Heaven? Did the Lord work it into his life for it to serve, one day, as a way to glorify God? Once again, I am not saying we are to sit down and take abuse. I am saying that when abuse in our lives happens, as it always does, can God transform it into something positive?

Joseph, son of the biblical patriarch Jacob, was a man whose actual life situation was similar to my Josh's. (See Genesis 37:39-46.) He was entrusted with many painful scenarios and called to glorify God in the forging fire of family hatred, abuse and attempted murder. He was to worship the King of Kings in and because of his forging. And when Joseph did, not only was God lifted high as sovereign: Joseph's obedience and worship had repercussions for God's ultimate out-working of world history through the Jewish nation!

As I have shown, God has freed, fired, and forged into vessels of worship many attitudes, actions and situations that have been encrusted within my heart over the course of my life. As long as they remained encrusted, trapped, they were separated from their intended use. But each of them has been entrusted to me for my worship of Jesus.

Vessels used for worship do not appear spontaneously: A gold vessel does not come into the service of the King without an extreme process of preparation. The metal has to be mined from within the darkness of the earth. Then it is extracted from the surrounding materials and fired to remove impurities. Next it is poured and beaten out to form and fashion a vessel. Then it must be chosen and sanctified. Work, forming and time must take place before it is suitable for service to worship.

This is how it is with all the treasures of darkness, the "good" that God brings out of "all things," even the black, difficult ones in our lives (Romans 8:28). Each of us has the power and choice, in God's hands, to turn our treasures of darkness into vessels of honor or dishonor.

God defines what worshiping Him looks like. Can worship really erupt from our sufferings? From tragedy? From life crises? From difficult situations?

I am a witness to the truth of worship emanating from the yielded heart of a beloved disciple. I have seen the power of thanking God and worshiping Him in the trials of my life. Submitting to His plan, receiving and allowing Him to refine the vessels intended for worship that He has entrusted to me, has flooded the halls of my life with amazing joy, peace and glory.

What will you do with the articles for worship with which God has entrusted you?

Deep Purpose

I could wrap this book with a huge bow by exposing some great personal hurdle. But that is not the point of sovereignty. Sovereignty is not an exposure of those who have wronged me, nor how I have so nobly endured someone's abuse. Sovereignty is about relinquishing my control and receiving my God in every aspect of my life.

Life is not an Easter egg hunt where I scour about collecting more and more happy moments. It will not end with me holding a basket of pleasures pried out of God's clenched fist. My end will be Him. My end is a collection of moments which culminated in my knowing God as my sovereign God. He is my moments. He is my Life. He is my eternal Reward!

Life is not a continuous and endless winter. Life has seasons. But just as certain winter conditions affect the success of a farmer's crops, we will miss the fruitfulness of our spiritual harvest if we resist our spiritual winter. Life contains the full gamut of the seasonal ebb and flow of existence, and if we cooperate with Him, God will use every aspect, every ebb and every flow, to increase the amount and quality of our harvest.

The way we live our lives reveals our motivation, our intent, and ultimately, our focus. Do we serve and seek the Lord, or ourselves? If we seek and serve ourselves, we will leave life in bitterness because life has not served us. But if our life intent is to know the Father, He will give us the grace to accept and receive ALL of life as from Him.

Sovereignty Forever

I could write about sovereignty forever, and probably will.

There is no end to this subject because there is no end to Him and His expression of Life. God's sovereignty is a vital aspect of His Lordship and an ever-expanding Truth into the mystery of His ways.

When someone confides in me, I do not expect him not to speak of the hardships he has experienced. I listen as the story unfolds and enjoy it in its totality.

In the same way, we must listen to our Author to hear His story in each of us. To live accepting God's sovereignty is to live listening. We hear God; it is not our job to tell Him. And to hear Him we must say "yes" to the whole of our Authored story and life. We are not called to live in what we deem acceptable ways and circumstances. We are called to live in Truth – the truth of our reality, the truth of our situations, the truth of God's choices. God is our Truth. He is our *end*.

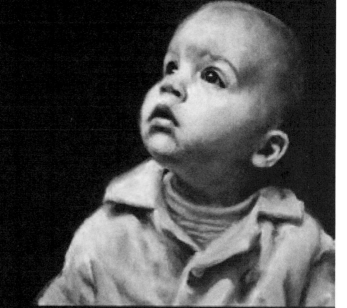

Want to read more from John Enslow?

Where are You, God?

We Seek the God Who Wants to be Found

Shulami✝e Ministries

READMK.COM
*Read articles, daily devotions and more on the
Online Library of Martha Kilpatrick.*

SHULAMITEPODCAST.COM
*Listen to the weekly Shulamite Podcast, and hear
unfiltered conversations about real life with Jesus.*

GETALONGWITHGOD.COM
*Interested in the ups and downs of discipleship?
A blog about discovering a God worth knowing.*

LIVINGCHRISTIANBOOKS.COM
*Shop for all things Martha Kilpatrick as well as
timeless classics by those who've gone before.*

THE SHULAMITE APP
*Tap into all the resources of Shulamite Ministries
while on-the-go with your iPhone and iPad.*

*Easy to use and mobile-friendly,
Shulamite.com houses our ministry's
latest podcasts, daily devotions, blog posts
and more. Stay up-to-date on ministry news, new
teachings by Martha, and all upcoming events by
making Shulamite.com a daily stop!*

**Here is a hub for the prodigals and the truth-seekers,
the brokenhearted and the hungry—all who would
discover a God worth knowing!**

SHULAMITE.COM